T0240853

Java EE Web Application Primer

Building Bullhorn: A Messaging App with JSP, Servlets, JavaScript, Bootstrap and Oracle

Dave Wolf

A.J. Henley

Apress®

Java EE Web Application Primer: Building Bullhorn: A Messaging App with JSP, Servlets, JavaScript, Bootstrap and Oracle

Dave Wolf
New York, USA

A.J. Henley
Washington, D.C., District of Columbia, USA

ISBN-13 (pbk): 978-1-4842-3194-4
ISBN-13 (electronic): 978-1-4842-3195-1
https://doi.org/10.1007/978-1-4842-3195-1

Library of Congress Control Number: 2017962002

Cover image by Freepik (www.freepik.com)

Managing Director: Welmoed Spahr
Editorial Director: Todd Green
Acquisitions Editor: Steve Anglin
Development Editor: Matthew Moodie
Technical Reviewer: Manuel Jordan Elera
Coordinating Editor: Mark Powers
Copy Editor: April Rondeau

Distributed to the book trade worldwide by Springer Science+Business Media New York, 233 Spring Street, 6th Floor, New York, NY 10013. Phone 1-800-SPRINGER, fax (201) 348-4505, email orders-ny@springer-sbm.com, or visit www.springeronline.com. Apress Media, LLC is a California LLC and the sole member (owner) is Springer Science + Business Media Finance Inc (SSBM Finance Inc). SSBM Finance Inc is a **Delaware** corporation.

For information on translations, please email rights@apress.com, or visit http://www.apress.com/rights-permissions.

Apress titles may be purchased in bulk for academic, corporate, or promotional use. eBook versions and licenses are also available for most titles. For more information, reference our Print and eBook Bulk Sales web page at http://www.apress.com/bulk-sales.

Any source code or other supplementary material referenced by the author in this book is available to readers on GitHub via the book's product page, located at www.apress.com/9781484231944. For more detailed information, please visit http://www.apress.com/source-code.

Printed on acid-free paper

To those who seek to teach themselves.

Table of Contents

About the Authors

Dave Wolf is a certified Project Management Professional (PMP) with over 20 years of experience as a software developer, analyst, and trainer. His latest projects include collaboratively developing training materials and programming bootcamps for Java and Python.

A.J. Henley is a technology educator with over 20 years of experience as a developer, designer, and systems engineer. He is an instructor at Howard University and Montgomery College.

About the Technical Reviewer

Manuel Jordan Elera is an autodidactic developer and researcher who enjoys learning new technologies for his own experiments and for creating new integrations.

Manuel won the 2010 Springy Award—Community Champion and Spring Champion 2013. In his little free time, he reads the Bible and composes music on his guitar. Manuel is known online as dr_pompeii. He has tech reviewed numerous books for Apress, including *Pro Spring Messaging* (2017), *Pro Spring, 4th Edition* (2014), *Practical Spring LDAP* (2013), *Pro JPA 2, Second Edition* (2013), and *Pro Spring Security* (2013).

Read his 13 detailed tutorials about many Spring technologies or contact him through his blog at `http://www.manueljordanelera.blogspot.com`. You can also follow him on his Twitter account, `@dr_pompeii`.

Introduction

Are you a Java developer wondering how to create an Enterprise application? Do you find the different components overwhelming or confusing, not knowing how they go together? We're here to help. What if you could just get an example application working and use that knowledge to continue your Java journey?

This book and the accompanying code will show you one way to create a website. It's not the only way. It may not be the best way for every application. But it's a way that will introduce you to the different components of Java Enterprise application development. And it's a good way to get started.

In *Java EE Web Application Primer*, you'll learn the basics of Java EE application development. You'll see how the parts connect. You will have the Java code for a complete, working application.

The Software

Our students take our courses to learn how to program for large companies. We have found these are the skills most requested by the companies hiring our students. We choose to use Java 8, Oracle 12c, and Eclipse for developing the application. Similarly, we choose to use JPA (Java Persistence API) instead of Hibernate. We choose JSTL (Java Standard Tag Library) over other available options. Again, these technologies teach core skills without hiding all the implementation details from the student. Our application is designed to teach. We provide the complete source code.

You will learn much simply by reviewing and modifying the source code. This book answers the questions you may have after working with the source code, and the source code helps explain how the concepts in this book have been implemented.

How to Use This Book

We wrote this book based on our experience teaching Java bootcamps and other programming courses. The objective of our courses is to help people learn skills they can use at work. Businesses care more about results than theory, and we apply that principle to our application. This book answers the questions many of our students have about web application development when starting out.

What Our Students Have Achieved

> *"I remember when the light bulbs started going off in my head, when the gibberish on the screen started to make sense. It was the most amazing feeling to start catching up with the rest of my impressive classmates."*
>
> —Vicky, now a project manager at a Fortune 100 company

> *"I went through four years of university schooling in computer science, and I can honestly say that going through this course gave me a wealth of experience that I only had a taste of during my schooling. I certainly had project experience under my belt graduating with a tech degree, but doing project after project with Dave and Alton, the instructors, really cemented the theory and practices I had learned previously in stone. More than that, I got to patch up a lot of holes that I had left unfilled from missed opportunities in college."*
>
> —Francis, now an analyst at a Fortune 100 company

If you're ready to get started and develop your first Java Enterprise web application, we thank you for choosing our book to begin your journey. Know that you will face challenges and frustrations. You aren't alone. We have found that as our students worked through those, they learned more about software development than we could ever teach in a book. You're in the right place. Wait no longer. It's time to move on to Chapter 1!

CHAPTER 1

Getting Started

VirtualBox allows you to create virtual computers within your physical computer, enabling you to run multiple computers on one system. Setting up VirtualBox requires very few steps. Once installed, you can then import an existing virtual computer and begin work using that system.

Click and run the file to install VirtualBox just like with any other software you've ever downloaded. If you are using Windows, double-click the setup file and follow the prompts to install. If you are using a Mac, open the DMG file that you downloaded and drag the VirtualBox file to your Applications folder. During the installation, keep all of the options set to their default.

Start the VirtualBox program. VirtualBox allows you to manage your various virtual machines and easily create new ones. You can run VirtualBox directly from the installation program, or you can start it from the desktop icon.

Note Download VirtualBox from Oracle's website: `http://www.oracle.com/technetwork/server-storage/virtualbox/downloads/index.html`

D. Wolf and A.J. Henley, *Java EE Web Application Primer*,
https://doi.org/10.1007/978-1-4842-3195-1_1

The Oracle Virtual Machine

Being lazy—I mean, efficient—we used a pre-built Oracle virtual machine (VM) image to develop the site. Oracle makes this VM available for download at no cost (registration required). The VM requires the open source VirtualBox software be installed on your computer as just described. The VM hosts the latest version of the Oracle database (version 12c). It also contains SQL Developer and even Java 1.8. You will only need to install Eclipse, which we'll cover in a later section.

Tip Download the Oracle Database Application Developer virtual machine from the Oracle website at `http://www.oracle.com/technetwork/database/enterprise-edition/databaseappdev-vm-161299.html`. You must accept the terms of the software prior to downloading.

Once you have the Oracle virtual machine file ready, select File ➤ Import Appliance in the menu bar. Click the Open Appliance button to select the Oracle virtual machine file. Navigate to the file with the .ova file extension. Selecting this file will open a dialog box in VirtualBox that displays the settings. You can select the Import button from here. The next window will show you the configuration of the current virtual appliance.

Once you click on Import, VirtualBox will copy the disk images and create a virtual machine with the settings described in the dialog. You will see the Oracle virtual machine in the VirtualBox Manager's list of virtual machines. The VirtualBox Manager is the first screen that opens when you open VirtualBox. Select your machine, click Start, and give it time to load, then you can work with that machine as if it were a separate computer.

Note If you're not using the Oracle virtual machine, you can complete everything in this book using Windows.

You can download and install Oracle database version 12c for Windows at `http://www.oracle.com/technetwork/database/enterprise-edition/downloads/database12c-win64-download-2297732.html`.

You will also need to install SQL Developer, which you can find at `http://www.oracle.com/technetwork/developer-tools/sql-developer/downloads/index.html`.

Finally, you will need to install Eclipse Oxygen from `http://www.eclipse.org/downloads`.

CHAPTER 2

What Is a Database?

A database is a place to permanently store data for retrieval in a safe, efficient way. A database allows us to create data and save it permanently. It allows us to retrieve previously created data, update existing data, or delete existing data.

A transaction groups SQL statements so that they are all applied to the database. If one statement fails for some reason, all the statements are undone from the database. Transactions ensure data integrity. Transactions distinguish a database management system such as Oracle from a file system.

The properties of a database transaction that ensure data validity are atomicity, consistency, isolation, and durability.

- *Atomicity* refers to the fact that in each database transaction either all the information is saved or none of the information is saved.
- *Consistency* ensures that a transaction either works correctly or the dataset is returned to the state it was in before the transaction was executed.
- *Isolation* refers to the ability of a database to keep a transaction that is not yet committed distinctly separate from the working database.

D. Wolf and A.J. Henley, *Java EE Web Application Primer*,
https://doi.org/10.1007/978-1-4842-3195-1_2

- *Durability* refers to the way committed data is saved by the system such that, even in the event of a failure and system restart, the data is available in its correct state.

The database stores data in sets, which are most commonly viewed as tables. One row of a database table represents a record containing related attributes, called *fields*. Fields are represented by the columns in a table.

Referential Integrity

Your database management system (DBMS) supports referential integrity. The goal of referential integrity is to avoid having "orphaned" data. Orphaned data can happen when you are deleting or updating the data in your tables; for example, if you have a post in your database that does not have a matching user. This shouldn't happen and is often the result of importing poorly formatted data or inadvertently deleting a user. A database management system such as Oracle can enforce referential integrity to prevent this by denying changes that will result in orphaned data.

Null Values

Sometimes there is no value in a column of a row. In this case, the column stores a NULL value. You can think of this as a flag to indicate the absence of data. NULL is different from the numeric value zero or a string with a length of zero characters. It is neither. It is nothing, because no value has been stored in the column for this record. NULL, it turns out, is very useful. You can search for a field in records that contain NULL and know that they are the ones with no value in the field.

Primary Keys, Foreign Keys, and Indexes

Databases are very powerful tools that allow us to search and sort data at incredible speeds. An essential ingredient of the mechanics of a database is that each record should be unique. To make each record unique, either use an existing field that is unique to each record or add a field to each record that contains a unique number.

Your DBMS can generate a unique number for each record. The unique number of each record becomes its primary key. This field distinguishes that record from any other in the table.

When a second table contains data related to that of the first table, the second table can refer to the original using the primary key field.

A primary key used as a reference in another table is called a foreign key. Foreign keys define a reference from one table (the child) to another table (the parent).

To make access to a column of data more efficient, the database will create an object called an *index*. An index contains an entry for each value in the indexed column(s), resulting in fast access to rows. Like an index in a print book, the database can look up the requested value in the index and quickly locate its corresponding row in the table.

Joining Tables

Relationships are a means to join data to different tables. This helps you avoid redundancy in the tables. You can divide your data into different tables—entering it only once—and then reference it from other tables by establishing relationships.

There are three types of relationships, as follows:

- A One-to-One relationship is where each record in the first table has only one matching record in the second table. This usually happens when information in one table is divided across multiple tables. This is not common.
- A One-to-Many relationship is where each record in the first table matches with multiple records in the second table. For example, a user can have multiple posts.
- A Many-to-Many relationship is where each record in the first table can have many corresponding records in the second table, and also each record in the second table can have many corresponding records in the first table.

Normalization

In a normalized data structure, each table contains information about a single entity and each piece of information is stored in exactly one place.

Normalization is the process of efficiently organizing data in a database. This is done by organizing the columns (fields or attributes) and tables of a relational database to minimize data redundancy.

The goals of the normalization process are to eliminate redundant data and ensure data dependencies make sense.

Structured Query Language (SQL)

A database has its own programming language, SQL (Structured Query Language). SQL is a nonprocedural language that provides database access. All database operations are performed using SQL. Java can talk to the database management system using SQL. This is done using the

JDBC API, which allows your application to specify which records to retrieve based on various criteria. For example, you can select records created between certain dates or update only records that meet given criteria. SQL can also be used to create database objects, such as user tables and saved queries, which are known as views. A view contains no data itself but is simply the stored query the use of which simplifies accessing the data.

SQL (pronounced as the letters S-Q-L or *sequel*) is a specialized database language that consists of statements that are very close to English. SQL has one purpose: to communicate with a database. We communicate with the database to add, update, or delete data. We also communicate with the database to create and modify tables and other database objects.

Almost every major DBMS supports SQL. Learning SQL will enable you to interact with almost every database you might encounter. SQL is easy to learn. The statements consist of descriptive English words. SQL is powerful. Cleverly using the language elements allows you to perform complex database operations. SQL is a standard governed by ANSI (American National Standards Institute). In addition to the standard implementation of SQL, most vendors implement their own proprietary extensions. The version of SQL) you use for Oracle may differ from the version you use to access other databases.

Working with the Oracle Database

Just as you use an IDE (integrated development environment) to work with Java programs, you can also use an IDE to work with Oracle databases. This IDE is called SQL Developer. The virtual machine has a copy of SQL Developer already installed.

How to Open and Use SQL Developer

To open SQL Developer in the virtual machine, simply click its icon on the desktop.

Tip Oracle provides step-by-step instructions for using SQL Developer on their technetwork website. If you use the virtual machine, then everything is installed for you. Browse to `http://www.oracle.com/webfolder/technetwork/tutorials/obe/db/sqldev/r40/sqldev4.0_GS/sqldev4.0_GS.html`.

CHAPTER 3

Installing and Running Eclipse

Your virtual machine contains all the software you need to create Bullhorn—the Oracle Database 12c, SQL Developer, and Java 1.8—but it doesn't contain the Eclipse IDE. You will need to download and install that yourself. Fortunately, the installation process is very easy.

INSTALL ECLIPSE ON THE VIRTUAL MACHINE

To install Eclipse on the virtual machine, you will need to open Firefox and download the Eclipse archive. Then, you will need to extract the files from the archive. Next, you will need to run the setup program that is included in the archive files. Finally, open Eclipse.

1. From the virtual machine, open the Firefox web browser. You can get to Firefox by clicking on the Applications menu and selecting the icon for Firefox Web Browser.
2. Next, browse to `http://www.eclipse.org/downloads`.
3. Click on the orange button to download Eclipse. You'll be installing the latest version, which is called Oxygen.
4. You'll be directed to another page with an orange Download button. Click this one as well.

D. Wolf and A.J. Henley, *Java EE Web Application Primer*,
https://doi.org/10.1007/978-1-4842-3195-1_3

5. Select the option to open with the Archive Manager when this window is displayed. The Archive Manager is the program that will extract your files.

6. You'll be prompted to select a folder into which you want to place the extracted files. Browse to the Home folder and select Extract.

7. Check the option to open the folder to view the files. Once you see the extracted files, look for the file called `eclipse-install`.

8. Select the option to install Eclipse for Java EE.

9. Your folder should be `/home/oracle/eclipse/jee-oxygen`.

10. Click Launch.

11. Accept the default workspace. This is where your project files will be kept.

You have just installed Eclipse Oxygen.

HOW TO CHANGE THE PORT IN TOMCAT

By default, Tomcat is configured to listen on the following port numbers: 8005, 8080, and 8009. The port we're most interested in is 8080 since it's used for HTTP access. When you run a web application in Eclipse using Tomcat, the URL becomes `http://localhost:8080/ApplicationName`. However, sometimes these ports are used by other software running on the computer. Fortunately, Eclipse makes it easy to change the port numbers.

1. From your web project, in the *Servers* view, double-click on the server name.
2. That will open a configuration page for Tomcat as follows:
3. Notice that the port numbers are shown in the table on the right. Click to edit; for example:
4. Once you change the port number for HTTP from 8080 to 9000, you should press `Ctrl + S` to save the change and restart the server.

Your application should now run without conflict. If you do get a conflict, then you've chosen another used port. Repeat the process with a different port number. It's best to select a port within the range of 1025 to 65535. You can research "Well-known port numbers" to find many articles explaining the reasoning here.

CHAPTER 4

Bullhorn Site Overview

The diagram in Figure 4-1 illustrates how the site fits together. Only the core components are shown. You may wish to add additional pages and classes as needed.

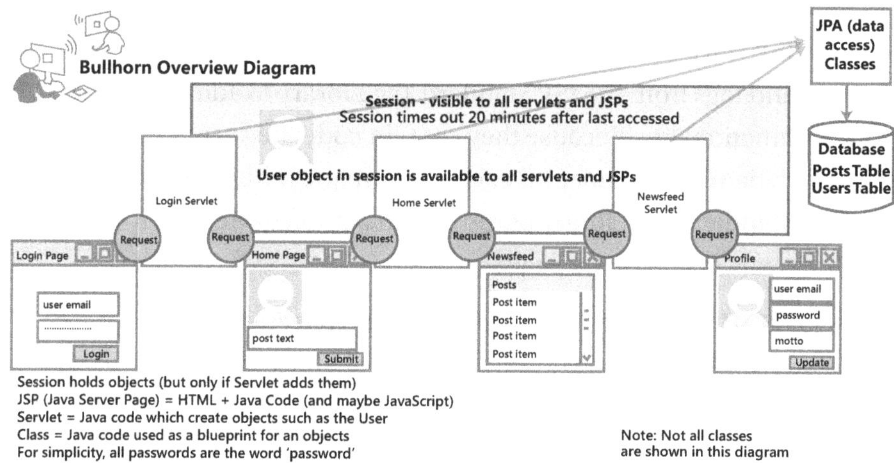

Figure 4-1. *The components that make up Bullhorn*

The Components of Bullhorn

- **Servlets** Java classes that extend the web server to provide an interface to the browser and database or other servlets.

D. Wolf and A.J. Henley, *Java EE Web Application Primer*,
https://doi.org/10.1007/978-1-4842-3195-1_4

- **JPA classes** Java Persistence API classes that are used to communicate between the servlets and the database.
- **Request objects** represent information sent between the browser and the servlets. This information might include email addresses and passwords that are being used by the servlet to allow access to the site.
- **Sessions** are the web server's method or approach of retaining data while the user is accessing the site.
- **User objects** The user information is stored in a class that will be stored in the session and is available to all pages for the current user.
- **JSP** (Java Server Pages) Web pages that contain HTML and tags from the JSP Standard Tag Library to add functionality. Because they contain code they can dynamically render for each user's request. The JSP Standard Tag Library permits each person to view their own version of the page.
- **HTML** (Hypertext Markup Language) pages. HTML is a system for tagging text files to control fonts, colors, and images on your web pages.

Tip To keep your HTML from getting too complicated, use CSS (Cascading Style Sheets) and JavaScript to control the presentation of your content and let HTML control the layout.

The Bullhorn application contains web pages for login, home, news feed, and user profile. The user starts at the login page. Once the user clicks the Login button, the request (data from the login form) will be sent to the login servlet.

The login servlet will validate the user against the database. A valid user will be stored in the session, which is the website's way of remembering data between page views. Invalid users will not get past the login page until they enter a correct username and password combination.

We will create other objects (classes) to validate data or support the classes and pages shown in the diagram.

What Does Each Page Look Like?

The login page will contain text boxes in which the user will enter their email and password. This information will be verified in the login servlet. If they match what is in the database then the user will be redirected to their home page. If they do not match then the user will be prompted to log in again. Users who reach the login page but aren't registered on the site can register for a login by clicking on the "Join" link. See Figure 4-2.

Figure 4-2. *The login page contains text boxes for email and password and a button to sign in to the application*

The home page will allow each user to create a new post. Each post is limited to 141 characters, so the home page enforces this restriction (see Figure 4-3). Once the user is logged in, all pages contain a navigation bar at the top that allows the user to navigate to different pages, view or edit their profile, and search for posts containing a specific word.

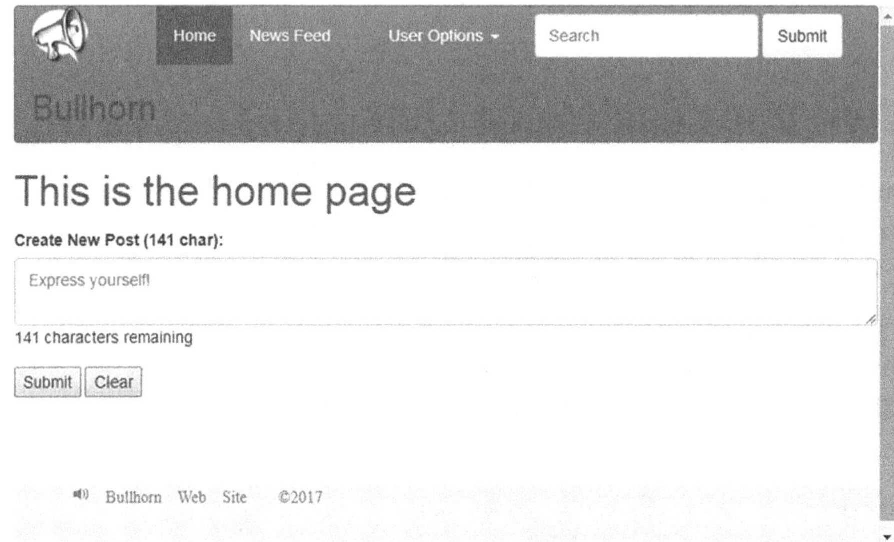

***Figure 4-3.** The home page contains a form to submit a post to the database. The form contains a text box and buttons to either submit the post or clear the form.*

Each page contains the same navigation bar, which allows the user to move around the application. The navigation bar contains the logo, links for the home page and the news feed page, and a search box. It also displays the name of the logged-in user. The user can also select from various user options, which is implemented as a drop-down list. These include logging out, viewing or editing profile, and submitting feedback. See Figure 4-4.

Figure 4-4. *The navigation bar in Bullhorn shows at the top of every page*

The "News Feed" link in the navigation bar will take a user to the news feed page, which displays all posts from all users. Each user's email address is a link that will display the user's profile information. Clicking Search in the navigation bar will also display the news feed, but filtered to posts that contain the text entered in the search text box. See Figure 4-5.

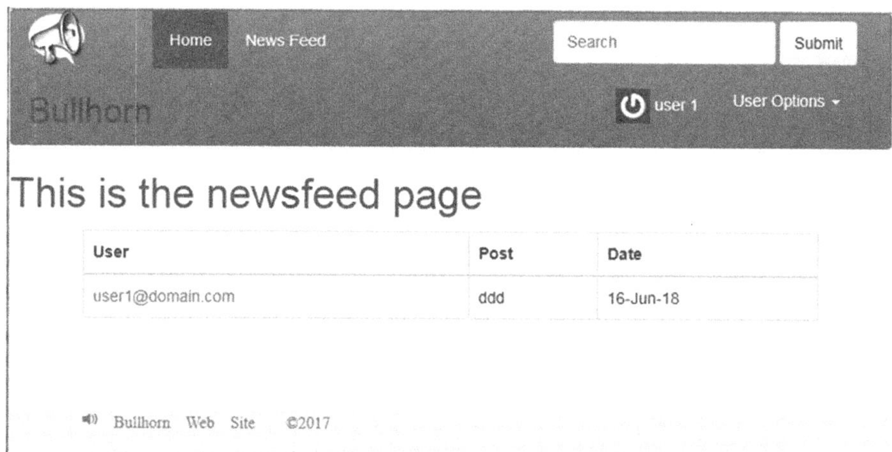

Figure 4-5. *The news feed page displays any posts that are in the database*

The profile for a user is read-only. It displays their email, motto, join date, and avatar image, if any. Users can view profiles for other users by clicking on their user names from the news feed page. See Figure 4-6.

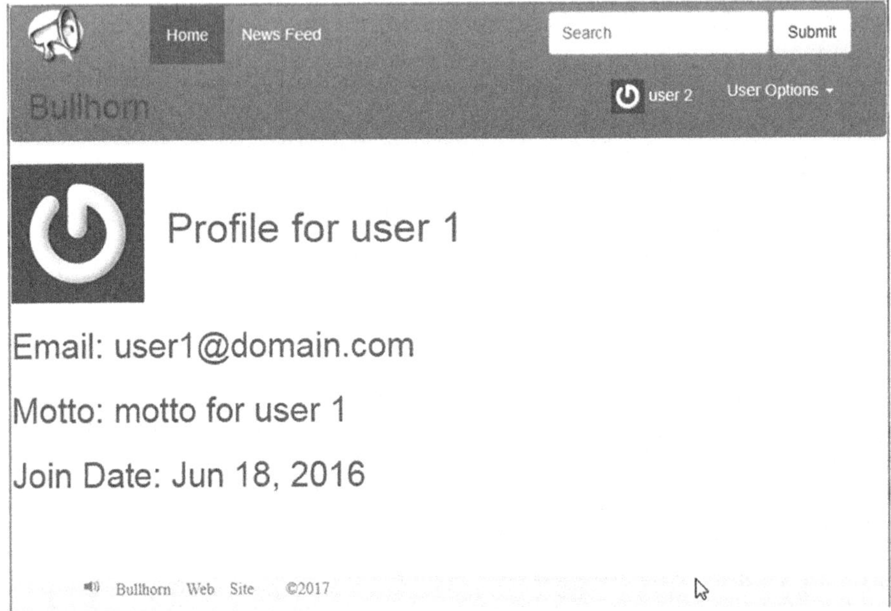

***Figure 4-6.** The profile page for a user shown in read-only view*

Editing a Profile

If a user views their own profile, then the profile can be edited. See Figure 4-7.

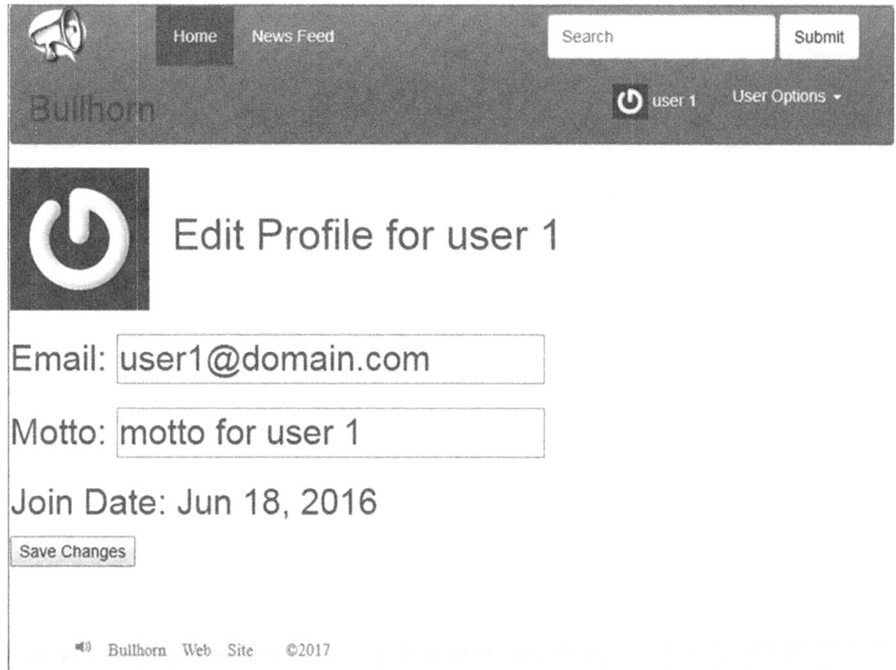

***Figure 4-7.** The profile page for the logged-in user displays with text boxes and a button so the user can make changes*

The support page doesn't show much, just some text to let you know it exists. We could modify this to include a text box that will send an email or add a record to the database. Then, the support person could check for new messages periodically. See Figure 4-8.

Figure 4-8. *The support page could allow you to let users submit requests to the web administrator*

CHAPTER 5

What Is MVC?

The model-view-controller (MVC) pattern is a software-design pattern used for creating data-driven web applications. A design pattern is a general solution that addresses common software-design challenges. While not a finished design, you may think of a design pattern as a template or set of best practices.

Following the MVC pattern means you intend to keep the presentation layer (view), business logic (controller), and database layer (model) separate. Changes made to one layer will minimally impact the others.

The real benefit of MVC is not seen when writing the code, but rather when maintaining it. Code is in independent units and can be maintained without keeping the entire application in your head.

Team building around MVC is easier. The design lends itself to segmentation among different people or groups. Imagine a View Team that is responsible for great views, a Model Team that knows all about the data, and a Controller Team that understands the application flow and business rules. Each can work on their part of the application concurrently without regard for the other teams. This allows for more rapid application development.

Another great advantage of MVC is code reuse. The application's logic implemented in the model and controller gets reused for each different view.

D. Wolf and A.J. Henley, *Java EE Web Application Primer*,
https://doi.org/10.1007/978-1-4842-3195-1_5

The Model, View, Controller, and Service in Bullhorn

When you think of the model, think of the database. Generally, the model is constructed first. The model must store the data. The model may consist of classes that communicate with the database. The model in Bullhorn is represented by the Oracle database and the entity classes, which represent the tables in Oracle.

Once you create the data model and any classes that are part of the model, move on to the services. The services are all the code that interacts with the model.

Next, move on to the controller. The controller is part of the web application and moves data between the services and the view. The controller also determines which page or servlet is called next. In Bullhorn, the servlets happen to also be the controller. This is not always the case. The controller is simply that code that controls application-specific logic. Since this is a web application, the servlets are in charge of getting data from the view and determining which JSP will display next. If you have Java classes that contain that functionality, they will be part of the controller.

The part of the application the user actually sees is called the *view*. It presents the data to the user and gets data from the user, which is then passed back to the model through the services and controller. The view in Bullhorn consists of JSPs (Java Server Pages) using Bootstrap, CSS (Cascading Style Sheets), JavaScript, and images. All the parts of the view work to create the pages that are displayed in the user's browser. See Figure 5-1.

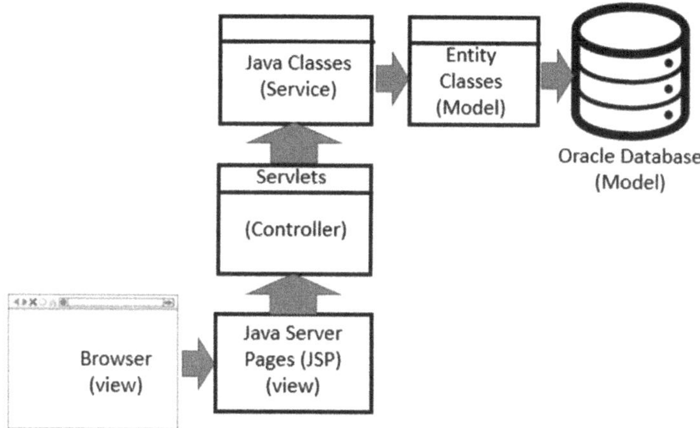

Figure 5-1. *The components of Bullhorn are logically divided into layers called Model, View, Controller, and Service*

Tip Perform validation in every layer. Data can come to your application through ways unanticipated by you when you initially develop it, not just through the browser. For example, it may come to be that you need to import information into your database. Or, you may later write a web service that interacts directly with your service layer.

CHAPTER 6

Creating a Web Application

We will create the Bullhorn application as a dynamic web project, which will allow us to develop it with HTML, JSP, servlets, and using JPA to connect to the database. If you understand what all those things are then you can stop reading now. If you're still with me, then those things will be explained as we go.

Our dynamic web application will contain not only static HTML pages but also dynamic Java Server Pages (JSPs) and servlets. We'll be able to pass data between the different parts of the application.

The database is actually a separate piece of software that your web application will communicate with. In many systems, the database actually resides on a different computer entirely. The JSPs will send information to the servlets. The servlets will send information to (and get information from) the database through the service layer. And the servlet will send the result back to the JSP.

Note It is possible to send information straight to the database from a JSP. It is also possible to send information between two JSPs. We won't do that here. We're putting a servlet in between every conversation. That allows us to intercept each message with some Java code in the servlet, which will make it easy to validate, evaluate, and redirect each intercepted message.

D. Wolf and A.J. Henley, *Java EE Web Application Primer*,
https://doi.org/10.1007/978-1-4842-3195-1_6

CREATE A DYNAMIC WEB PROJECT USING ECLIPSE

Eclipse is preconfigured for various types of projects. I find the Dynamic Web Project most helpful. Starting one only consists of a few simple steps.

1. From Eclipse choose `File` ➤ `New` ➤ `Dynamic Web Project`.

   Give it a project name, such as `SampleDynamicWebProject`, as shown in Step 2.

2. Select the target runtime as Tomcat v.8.0 or higher. You may be prompted to install Tomcat before you can continue.

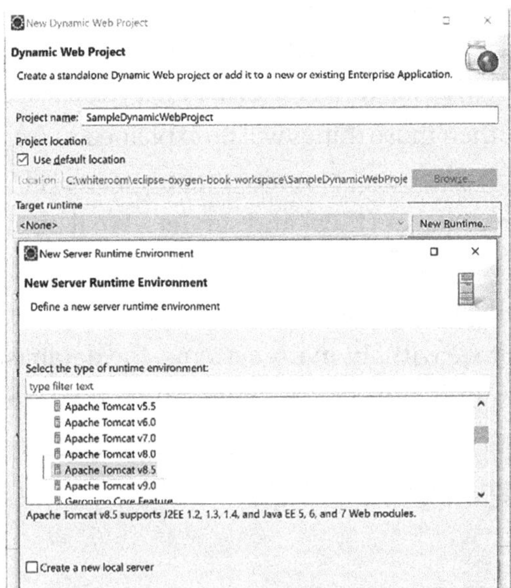

3. Click Finish.

4. If prompted, select “Yes” to associate with a Java EE Perspective.

5. Once your project contains some web pages, you can start them by selecting the page in the Project Explorer, then right-click and select `Run As` ➤ `Run on Server`. Your application will start in Eclipse.

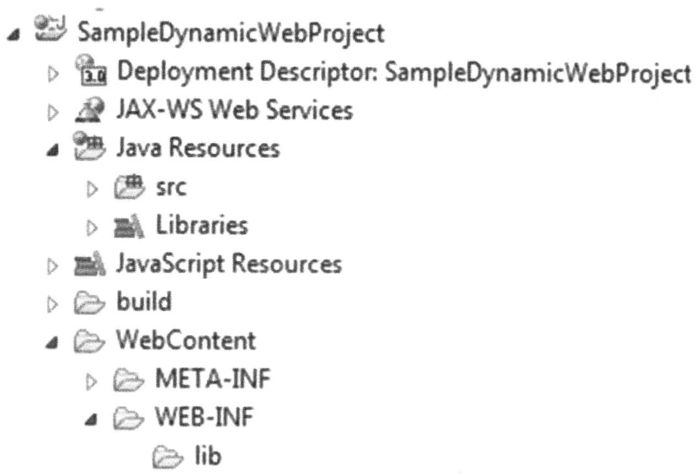

- SampleDynamicWebProject
  - Deployment Descriptor: SampleDynamicWebProject
  - JAX-WS Web Services
  - Java Resources
    - src
    - Libraries
  - JavaScript Resources
  - build
  - WebContent
    - META-INF
    - WEB-INF
      - lib

Figure 6-1. *The folder structure of a dynamic web project in Eclipse*

The dynamic web project generates folders for organizing Java code (see Figure 6-1). The most important are the Java source folder and the web content folder. Java servlets and classes should be placed in the `src` folder shown under Java Resources. JSP files belong in the `WebContent` folder. JSP files must not be placed in `WEB-INF` or they will not be accessible by your application. Use the `lib` folder under `WEB-INF` for JAR (Java Archive) files. We'll work with JAR files when we add the database to our project.

Tip The JAR (Java Archive) files for Bullhorn can be found in `WebContent/WEB-INF/lib`. You should copy all the JAR files in Bullhorn to the `/WEB-INF/lib` directory for any Dynamic Web Application you choose to develop.

CHAPTER 7

The DAO/Repository

Bullhorn requires two tables, for users and posts. We'll create these tables in Oracle and call them `Bhuser` and `Bhpost`, respectively. The user table will need the following fields: user name, user email, password, motto, and join date. The posts table will contain fields for post text, post date, and the ID of the user who created the post. Each table will also contain an ID field to uniquely identify each record. We can instruct SQL Developer to construct the tables by running scripts. Simply enter the text seen in Listing 7-1 in SQL Developer inside a new SQL worksheet.

Listing 7-1. The Data Definition for the Bhuser Table

```
CREATE TABLE BHUSER
 ("BHUSERID" NUMBER GENERATED BY DEFAULT ON NULL AS IDENTITY
 MINVALUE 1 MAXVALUE 9999999999999999999999999999 INCREMENT
 BY 1 START WITH 1 CACHE 20 NOORDER NOCYCLE ,
      "USERNAME" VARCHAR2(50 BYTE) NOT NULL,
      "USERPASSWORD" VARCHAR2(50 BYTE),
      "MOTTO" VARCHAR2(100 BYTE) NOT NULL,
      "USEREMAIL" VARCHAR2(100 BYTE) NOT NULL,
      "JOINDATE" DATE NOT NULL,
       PRIMARY KEY ("BHUSERID")
 ) ;
```


D. Wolf and A.J. Henley, *Java EE Web Application Primer*,
https://doi.org/10.1007/978-1-4842-3195-1_7

Now that we have a place to store our users, we can add another table in which to store the posts. The SQL for creating the Bhpost table is shown in Listing 7-2. You will enter that in SQL Developer in a SQL worksheet. Many developers use the same SQL worksheet and enter each table one below the other. Once the SQL is in a SQL worksheet, highlight the statements and press the CTRL and Enter keys together. Create the Bhuser table first since the Bhpost table contains a foreign key representing the BhuserId in the Bhuser table.

Listing 7-2. SQL for Creating the Bhpost Table

```
CREATE TABLE BHPOST
  ("POSTID" NUMBER GENERATED BY DEFAULT ON NULL AS IDENTITY
  MINVALUE 1 MAXVALUE 9999999999999999999999999999 INCREMENT
  BY 1 START WITH 1 CACHE 20 NOORDER NOCYCLE ,
       "POSTDATE" DATE NOT NULL,
       "POSTTEXT" VARCHAR2(141 BYTE) NOT NULL,
       "BHUSERID" NUMBER NOT NULL,
        PRIMARY KEY ("POSTID")
  );
```

Next, you may wish to enter some test data. Listings 7-3 and 7-4 show a few statements you can run. Enter the SQL into SQL Developer, highlight the statements, and press CTRL + Enter.

Listing 7-3. SQL Statements for Entering Test Data for the Bhuser Table

```
Insert into BHUSER (USERNAME,USERPASSWORD,MOTTO,USEREMAIL,JOI
NDATE) values ('user 1','password','motto for user 1','user1@
domain.com',to_date('18-JUN-16','DD-MON-RR'));
Insert into BHUSER (USERNAME,USERPASSWORD,MOTTO,USEREMAIL,JOI
NDATE) values ('user 2','password','motto for user 2','user2@
domain.com',to_date('22-JUL-15','DD-MON-RR'));
```

```
Insert into BHUSER (USERNAME,USERPASSWORD,MOTTO,USEREMAIL,JOI
NDATE) values ('user 3','password','motto for user 3','user3@
domain.com',to_date('31-DEC-16','DD-MON-RR'));
Insert into BHUSER (USERNAME,USERPASSWORD,MOTTO,USEREMAIL,JOI
NDATE) values ('user 4','password','motto for user 4','user4@
domain.com',to_date('22-JAN-17','DD-MON-RR'));

-- commit saves the data to the database
commit;
```

Listing 7-4. SQL Statements for Entering Test Data for the Bhpost Table

```
Insert into BHPOST (POSTDATE,POSTTEXT,BHUSERID) values (to_
date('18-JUN-17','DD-MON-RR'),'This is a test post',1);
Insert into BHPOST (POSTDATE,POSTTEXT,BHUSERID) values (to_
date('21-AUG-17','DD-MON-RR'),'Bullhorn is a fun program!',2);
Insert into BHPOST (POSTDATE,POSTTEXT,BHUSERID) values
(to_date('30-JUL-17','DD-MON-RR'),'Hello, I am posting
something',2);

-- commit saves the data to the database
commit;
```

If you need to recreate the tables, you can just delete them by running the following two lines in a SQL worksheet (Listing 7-5).

Listing 7-5. SQL Statements for Deleting Existing Table and Data

```
DROP TABLE BHPOST;
DROP TABLE BHUSER;
```

Now that you have your tables created and some test data entered in Oracle, it's time to go back to Eclipse and connect your project to the database. We'll use the Java Persistence API (JPA) for this.

Implement Java Persistence (JPA)

The Java Persistence API (JPA) is a set of standards that specify how Java will connect to a database using entities, also known as POJO (plain old Java objects). Each entity represents a single row in our database table. JPA treats the database objects as Java objects. Our program simply interacts with the entity, which in turn interacts with the database.

Sometimes we have a table that contains data from other tables. For example, a post in the Bullhorn table will contain a user ID that identifies the user who submitted the post. With JPA, the ID is replaced with the entire `User` object, allowing you to access all the data about the user from the `Post` entity.

JPA allows you to use your object-oriented programming skills to work with a database. Furthermore, it makes all databases look the same to your program. JPA is an object-relational mapping specification. It takes care of the details of connecting to the database. You set the values of various parameters for your existing database, and JPA will do the rest. The Eclipse JPA tools examine the tables and create a class for each. The class name is based on the table name. We will use Eclipse JPA tools to create the class and its getters and setters. The class fields map to the table fields. Each class represents one table in your database. An instance of a class represents one record, or row, in the table. The Eclipse JPA tools will handle sequences and identity keys. They will also handle table relationships. When your table contains a foreign key to another record in another table in the database, your class will contain an instance of the object representing the foreign key's table. For example, a `userID` column in your `Posts` table becomes a `User` object embedded in your `Posts` class.

An advantage of using JPA is that we can change the database without changing our Java code. The database information is stored in an XML file, which can be edited without recompiling your application. You may start off writing your application using MySQL, then as it grows move up to Oracle without any changes to your application code.

Queries in JPA are written in a language called JPQL (Java Persistence Query Language). This language is the same for all databases.

To implement JPA we need to configure a file called the `persistence.xml`. This file must be found under the Java source code folder in a folder called `META-INF`. Eclipse uses that configuration to generate the entity classes. After that, we will create helper classes for our application.

The first step is to copy three JAR files to the `WEB-INF\lib` folder of your project. The JAR files for this project are included with the code download. They can also be found in the `WEB-INF\lib` folder of the Bullhorn application. The JAR files are called `eclipselink.jar`, `javax.persistence_2.1.0.v201304241213.jar`, and `ojdbc6.jar`.

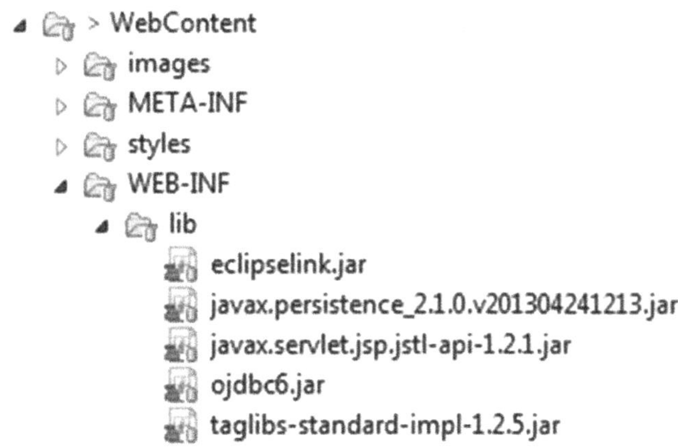

Note Place the following JAR files in the `WEB-INF\lib` folder: `eclipselink.jar`, `javax.persistence_2.1.0.v201304241213.jar`, and `ojdbc6.jar`. Any other location may not work. You may include the other JAR files you find in Bullhorn at the same time. We'll use them later.

The Persistence.xml File

To configure JPA, we need to create the `persistence.xml` file. In Eclipse, there are a few ways to create such a file, but we will create it in the `src` directory called `META-INF`. This particular location is required by the JPA specification. It can be any text file, which you will fill in with the values shown in Table 7-1. Don't feel like typing it all? You can copy the file from the download that accompanies this book. The values you need to change are detailed in the table. You may need to modify them as shown.

Table 7-1. *Settings for the Elements of the Bullhorn persistence.xml File*

XML Tag Name	Recommended Value
Persistence Unit Name	Bullhorn
Transaction Type	RESOURCE_LOCAL
Provider	org.eclipse.persistence.jpa.PersistenceProvider
Class	List once for each table in your database. So there should be two class elements: model.Bhuser and model.Bhpost
Exclude Unlisted Classes	False
Java.persistence.jdbc.url	`jdbc:oracle:thin:@localhost:1521:ora1`
javax.persistence.jdbc.user	system
javax.persistence.jdbc.password	password
javax.persistence.jdbc.driver	`oracle.jdbc.OracleDriver`

Listing 7-6 shows the full `persistence.xml` file.

Listing 7-6. Example persistence.xml File That Details All the JPA Settings

```
<?xml version="1.0" encoding="UTF-8"?>
<persistence version="2.1" xmlns=
"http://xmlns.jcp.org/xml/ns/persistence" xmlns:xsi=
"http://www.w3.org/2001/XMLSchema-instance" xsi:schemaLocation=
"http://xmlns.jcp.org/xml/ns/persistence http://xmlns.jcp.org/
xml/ns/persistence/
persistence_2_1.xsd">

<persistence-unit name="Bullhorn"
transaction-type="RESOURCE_LOCAL">
<provider>
org.eclipse.persistence.jpa.PersistenceProvider
</provider>
<class>model.Bhpost</class>
<class>model.Bhuser</class>
<exclude-unlisted-classes>
False
</exclude-unlisted-classes>

<properties>
<property name="javax.persistence.jdbc.url"
value="jdbc:oracle:thin:@localhost:1521:ora1"/>

<property name="javax.persistence.jdbc.user" value="system"/>

<property name="javax.persistence.jdbc.driver" value="oracle.
jdbc.OracleDriver"/>
```

```
<property name="javax.persistence.jdbc.password"
value="password"/>
</properties>
</persistence-unit></persistence>
```

Remember The `peristence.xml` file belongs in the `META-INF` directory found below the `src` directory. This location is required.

Once you have your `persistence.xml` file set up, you are ready to let Eclipse automatically generate the entities from the tables in your database. To do this, right-click on the project name and select "New." Then, navigate to the JPA menu for JPA Entities from Tables. The resulting dialog box will use the information in your `persistence.xml` file to connect to the database and generate a Java class for each table. Your program will use these Java classes (and the `persistence.xml` file) to find, add, edit, and delete records in the database.

The JPA Entities

```
package model;

import java.io.Serializable;
import javax.persistence.*;
import java.util.Date;
import java.util.List;

@Entity
@NamedQuery(name="Bhuser.findAll", query="SELECT b FROM Bhuser b")
public class Bhuser implements Serializable {
        private static final long serialVersionUID = 1L;
```

```
@Id
@GeneratedValue(strategy=GenerationType.IDENTITY)
private long bhuserid;

@Temporal(TemporalType.DATE)
private Date joindate;

private String motto;
private String useremail;
private String username;
private String userpassword;

//bi-directional many-to-one association to Bhpost
@OneToMany(mappedBy="bhuser")
private List<Bhpost> bhposts;

public Bhuser() {
}
public long getBhuserid() {
        return this.bhuserid;
}
public void setBhuserid(long bhuserid) {
        this.bhuserid = bhuserid;
}
public Date getJoindate() {
        return this.joindate;
}
public void setJoindate(Date joindate) {
        this.joindate = joindate;
}
public String getMotto() {
        return this.motto;
}
```

```
        public void setMotto(String motto) {
                this.motto = motto;
        }
        public String getUseremail() {
                return this.useremail;
        }
        public void setUseremail(String useremail) {
                this.useremail = useremail;
        }
        public String getUsername() {
                return this.username;
        }
        public void setUsername(String username) {
                this.username = username;
        }
        public String getUserpassword() {
                return this.userpassword;
        }
        public void setUserpassword(String userpassword) {
                this.userpassword = userpassword;
        }
        public List<Bhpost> getBhposts() {
                return this.bhposts;
        }
        public void setBhposts(List<Bhpost> bhposts) {
                this.bhposts = bhposts;
        }
        public Bhpost addBhpost(Bhpost bhpost) {
                getBhposts().add(bhpost);
                bhpost.setBhuser(this);

                return bhpost;
```

```
        }
        public Bhpost removeBhpost(Bhpost bhpost) {
                getBhposts().remove(bhpost);
                bhpost.setBhuser(null);
                return bhpost;
        }
}

package model;

import java.io.Serializable;
import javax.persistence.*;
import java.math.BigDecimal;
import java.util.Date;

@Entity
@NamedQuery(name="Bhpost.findAll",
     query="SELECT b FROM Bhpost b")
public class Bhpost implements Serializable {
        private static final long serialVersionUID = 1L;

        @Id
        @GeneratedValue(strategy=GenerationType.IDENTITY)
        private long postid;
        @Temporal(TemporalType.DATE)
        private Date postdate;
        private String posttext;

        //bi-directional many-to-one association to Bhuser
        @ManyToOne
        @JoinColumn(name="BHUSERID")
        private Bhuser bhuser;
        public Bhpost() {
        }
```

```
	public long getPostid() {
		return this.postid;
	}
	public void setPostid(long postid) {
		this.postid = postid;
	}
	public Date getPostdate() {
		return this.postdate;
	}
	public void setPostdate(Date postdate) {
		this.postdate = postdate;
	}
	public String getPosttext() {
		return this.posttext;
	}
	public void setPosttext(String posttext) {
		this.posttext = posttext;
	}
	public Bhuser getBhuser() {
		return this.bhuser;
	}

	public void setBhuser(Bhuser bhuser) {
		this.bhuser = bhuser;
	}
}
```

CHAPTER 8

The Service Layer

Your application will interact with the DAO through the service layer.

Create a DbUtilities Class

Every time your application connects to the database, it will execute the same code. You can make your application more efficient by creating a class of reusable methods that you can call as needed. Create a class called `DbUtilities`. This will allow you to simplify calling the Entity Manager when you need to read or write to the database. This class will be static (no instantiation required). It will have one method, `getFactory()`. It will return an instance of EntityManagerFactory as identified in the `persistence.xml`. See Listing 8-1.

Listing 8-1. The code listing for the DbUtilities Class

```
//DbUtil.java
package service;

import javax.persistence.EntityManager;
import javax.persistence.Persistence;

public class DbUtil {
        public static EntityManager getEntityManager(String s)
{
```


D. Wolf and A.J. Henley, *Java EE Web Application Primer*,
https://doi.org/10.1007/978-1-4842-3195-1_8

```
                return
                Persistence.createEntityManagerFactory(s).
                createEntityManager();
        }
}
//End of DbUtil.java
```

Create the DbUser Class

The DbUser class contains methods for working with the user. DbPost contains methods for working with the posts. Both classes are very similar, so only select methods from DbUser are shown here.

```
//DbUser.java
package service;

import javax.persistence.EntityManager;
import javax.persistence.EntityTransaction;
import javax.persistence.NoResultException;
import javax.persistence.TypedQuery;

import service.util.MD5Util;
import model.Bhuser;

/**
 * @author djw
 * DbUser class contains helper methods for working with Bhusers
 *
 */
public class DbUser {
/**
 * Gets a Bhuser from the database
 * @param userID - primary key from database. Must be type long
 * @return Bhuser
 */
```

```
public static Bhuser getUser(long userID)
{
        EntityManager em = DbUtil.getEntityManager
        ("Bullhorn");
        Bhuser user = em.find(Bhuser.class, userID);
        return user;
}

public static void insert(Bhuser bhUser) {
        EntityManager em = DbUtil.getEntityManager
        ("Bullhorn");
        EntityTransaction trans = em.getTransaction();
        try {
                trans.begin();
                em.persist(bhUser);
                trans.commit();
        } catch (Exception e) {
                e.printStackTrace();
                trans.rollback();
        } finally {
                em.close();
        }
}
/**
 * Gets a Gravatar URL given the email and size
 * In accordance with Gravatar's requirements the email
   will be hashed
 * with the MD5 hash and returned as part of the url
 * The url will also include the s=xx attribute to
   request a Gravatar of a
 * particular size.
 * References: <a href="http://www.gravatar.
   com">http://www.gravatar.com</>
```

```
 * @param email - email of the user who's gravatar
   you want
 * @param size - indicates pixel height of the image to
   be returned. Height and Width are same.
 * @return - the gravatar URL. You can test it in a
   browser.
 */
public static String getGravatarURL(String email,
Integer size){
        StringBuilder url = new StringBuilder();
        url.append("http://www.gravatar.com/avatar/");
        url.append(MD5Util.md5Hex(email));
        url.append("?s=" + size.toString());
        return url.toString();
}
/**
 * Updates the data in a Bhuser
 * Pass the method a Bhuser with all the values set to
   your liking and
 * this method will update the database with these
   values.
 * This method doesn't actually return anything but the
   good feeling
 * that your update has been completed. If it can't be
   completed then
 * it won't tell you. Sounds like something needs to be
   added in the future. Hmmm.
 * @param bhUser
 */
public static void update(Bhuser bhUser) {
        EntityManager em = DbUtil.getEntityManager
        ("Bullhorn");
```

```
        EntityTransaction trans = em.getTransaction();
        try {
                trans.begin();
                em.merge(bhUser);
                trans.commit();
        } catch (Exception e) {
                System.out.println(e);
                trans.rollback();
        } finally {
                em.close();
        }
}

/**
 * Removes a Bhuser from the database.
 * Not sure why you'd want to delete a Bhuser from the
   database but this
 * method will do it for you. This method does not
   explicitly remove the user's
 * posts, but most likely you've set up the database
   with cascading deletes, which
 * will take care of that. Gives no feedback.
 * @param bhUser that you never want to see again
 */
public static void delete(Bhuser bhUser) {
        EntityManager em = DbUtil.getEntityManager
        ("Bullhorn");
        EntityTransaction trans = em.getTransaction();
        try {
                trans.begin();
                em.remove(em.merge(bhUser));
                trans.commit();
```

```
        } catch (Exception e) {
                System.out.println(e);
                trans.rollback();
        } finally {
                em.close();
        }
}

/**
 * Gets a user given their email address.
 * You've got the email when they log in but you really
   need the
 * user and all its related information. This method
   will find the user
 * matching that email. The database should ensure that
   you can't have two users
 * with the same email. Otherwise there's no telling
   what you'd get.
 * @param email
 * @return Bhuser with that unique email address
 */
public static Bhuser getUserByEmail(String email)
{
        EntityManager em = DbUtil.getEntityManager
        ("Bullhorn");
        String qString = "Select u from Bhuser u "
                        + "where u.useremail
                          =:useremail";
        TypedQuery<Bhuser> q = em.createQuery(qString,
        Bhuser.class);
        q.setParameter("useremail", email);
        Bhuser user = null;
```

```
        try {
                System.out.println("Getting single user");
                 user = q.getSingleResult();
                 System.out.println(user.getUsername());
        }catch (NoResultException e){
                 System.out.println(e);
        }finally{
                 em.close();
        }
        return user;

}

/**
 * Is this user valid? This method has the answer for
   you.
 * Checks the database and counts the number of users
   with this
 * username and password. If it returns 0 then either
   the username
 * or password don't exist in the database. If it
   returns 1 then you have found
 * the user with that username and password. If it
   returns >1 then you need to
 * fix your database.
 * @param userEmail and userPassword
 * @return true or false indicating the user exists or
  doesn't
 */
public static boolean isValidUser(String userEmail,
String userPassword)
{
```

```
                EntityManager em =
                                DbUtil.
                                getEntityManager("Bullhorn");
                String qString = "Select count(b.bhuserid) from
                Bhuser b "
                        + "where b.useremail = :useremail and
                          b.userpassword = :userpass";
                TypedQuery<Long> q =
                em.createQuery(qString,Long.class);
                boolean result = false;
                q.setParameter("useremail", userEmail);
                q.setParameter("userpass", userPassword);

                try{
                        long userId = q.getSingleResult();
                        if (userId > 0)
                        {
                                result = true;
                        }
                }catch (Exception e){

                        result = false;
                }
                finally{
                                em.close();
                }
                return result;

        }

}
//End of DbUser.java
```

Create the DbPost Class

```
//DbPost.java
package service;

import java.util.List;
import javax.persistence.EntityManager;
import javax.persistence.EntityTransaction;
import javax.persistence.TypedQuery;
import model.Bhpost;

public class DbPost {

        public static void insert(Bhpost bhPost) {
                EntityManager em = DbUtil.getEntityManager
                ("Bullhorn");
                EntityTransaction trans = em.getTransaction();
                try {
                        trans.begin();
                        em.persist(bhPost);
                        trans.commit();
                } catch (Exception e) {
                        System.out.println(e.getMessage());
                        trans.rollback();
                } finally {
                        em.close();
                }
        }

        public static void update(Bhpost bhPost) {
                EntityManager em = DbUtil.getEntityManager
                ("Bullhorn");
                EntityTransaction trans = em.getTransaction();
```

```
        try {
                trans.begin();
                em.merge(bhPost);
                trans.commit();
        } catch (Exception e) {
                trans.rollback();
        } finally {
                em.close();
        }
}
public static void delete(Bhpost bhPost) {
        EntityManager em = DbUtil.getEntityManager
        ("Bullhorn");
        EntityTransaction trans = em.getTransaction();
        try {
                trans.begin();
                em.remove(em.merge(bhPost));
                trans.commit();
        } catch (Exception e) {
                System.out.println(e);
                trans.rollback();
        } finally {
                em.close();
        }
}
public static List<Bhpost> bhPost (){
        EntityManager em = DbUtil.getEntityManager
        ("Bullhorn");
        String qString = "select b from Bhpost b";

        List<Bhpost> posts = null;
        try{
```

```
            TypedQuery<Bhpost> query = em.create
             Query(qString,Bhpost.class);
            posts = query.getResultList();

    }catch (Exception e){
            e.printStackTrace();
    }
    finally{
                    em.close();
            }
    return posts;
}

public static List<Bhpost> postsofUser(long userid)
{
    EntityManager em = DbUtil.getEntityManager("Bul
    lhorn");
    List<Bhpost> userposts = null;
    String qString = "select b from Bhpost b where
    b.bhuser.bhuserid = :userid";

    try{
            TypedQuery<Bhpost> query = em.create
            Query(qString,Bhpost.class);
            query.setParameter("userid", userid);
            userposts = query.getResultList();
    }catch (Exception e){
            e.printStackTrace();
    }
    finally{
                    em.close();
            }
    return userposts;
}
```

```
public static List<Bhpost> postsofUser(String useremail)
{
        EntityManager em = DbUtil.getEntityManager
        ("Bullhorn");
        List<Bhpost> userposts = null;
        String qString = "select b from Bhpost b "
                        + "where b.bhuser.useremail =
                          :useremail";

        try{
                TypedQuery<Bhpost> query = em.create
                Query(qString,Bhpost.class);
                query.setParameter("useremail",
                useremail);
                userposts = query.getResultList();
        }catch (Exception e){
                e.printStackTrace();
        }
        finally{
                        em.close();
                }
        return userposts;
}

public static List<Bhpost> searchPosts (String search)
{
        EntityManager em = DbUtil.getEntityManager
        ("Bullhorn");
        List<Bhpost> searchposts = null;
        String qString = "select b from Bhpost b "
                        + "where b.posttext like
                          :search";
```

```
            try{
                    TypedQuery<Bhpost> query = em.create
                    Query(qString,Bhpost.class);
                    query.setParameter("search", "%" +
                    search + "%");
                    searchposts = query.getResultList();
            }catch (Exception e){
                    e.printStackTrace();
            }finally{
                    em.close();
            }return searchposts;
        }

}
//End of DbPost.java
```

CHAPTER 9

The Controller

The controller layer in our application contains code to handle application-specific logic. This includes concerns such as receiving data from web pages, sending data to the classes in the service layer, and sending the user the next servlet or JSP as appropriate. The controller does not access the database directly. The controller finds out what needs to be done, then finds the right class in the service layer or presentation layer and calls on that class to do its work. In our application, most of the code for the controller resides in Java servlets.

What Is a Servlet?

Servlets are Java classes that respond to incoming HTTP requests. The request is sent by the browser whenever you browse to a URL or submit a form. Servlets reside within the web server—Tomcat—and listen for requests. Then, they spring into action and process the request. Think of "operators are standing by!" When you create a servlet you are actually extending the functionality of the servlet container, Tomcat. Think of Tomcat as a web server that knows how to work with servlets and JSP files in addition to HTML.

The URL (web address) of your servlet will look something like `http://localhost:8080/webTest/SimpleServlet`, where `localhost` is the name representing your computer, `8080` is the port number, `webTest` is the application (or project) name, and `SimpleServlet` is the servlet URL as indicated in the servlet's `@WebServlet` annotation.

D. Wolf and A.J. Henley, *Java EE Web Application Primer*,
https://doi.org/10.1007/978-1-4842-3195-1_9

The servlet code in Listing 9-1 features a servlet that can be found at the SimpleServlet URL as specified in the @WebServlet attribute. It contains no code to process a request, only showing the structure. A servlet contains two methods, doGet and doPost. Each corresponds to the get or post method of a form. When the form is submitted, the method attribute of the form tag should be set to GET if you are only using the form values to retrieve read-only data such as another web page. If the web form is using GET, the data is transferred within the URL. You can see the parameter and its values in the URL following a ? symbol. This allows the user to copy and paste a link and get the same results again.

When submitting data to the server for entry into the database, you should use the POST method. POST does not use the URL to submit data. The parameters and values are transferred to the server in a package of data. This has several advantages, including the fact that the form and its submitted data cannot be bookmarked. Using POST also allows a form to submit larger quantities of data.

Listing 9-1. A Simple Web Servlet (Excluding Import Statements)

```
@WebServlet("/SimpleServlet")
public class SimpleServlet
                extends HttpServlet {

   protected void doGet(
                HttpServletRequest request,
                    HttpServletResponse response)
                throws ServletException, IOException {
        //code to handle GET requests goes here
        }

   protected void doPost(
                HttpServletRequest request,
                    HttpServletResponse response)
```

```
            throws ServletException, IOException {
        //code to handle POST requests goes here
        }
}
```

Getting the Form Data into the Servlet

When the user clicks the Submit button, the data from the form gets sent to the servlet in the request object. The web server takes care of this. The servlet container, Tomcat, will make the request object available to your servlet. Your input, named `userName`, will contain the name that the user has typed. The servlet can read that name by using the following code:

```
//set a variable with the value from the request
String userEmail = request.getParameter("userEmail");
```

Sending the Data to the Next Page

You can add any data (including objects such as `ArrayLists`) to the request or session. These will be available to the next page the servlet calls. Note that the request packet from the incoming request will not remain in scope, so it's necessary to put the data back into a new request packet.

```
//put the value back in the servlet's request
request.setAttribute("userEmail", userEmail);
```

Now the servlet has the data in a variable called `userEmail`. You're just writing Java code now, so you can work with it however you see fit. We'll use the `userEmail` and `userPassword` variables to hold the data and then validate that they match our expectations. At first we'll just create a method to validate known values. Later, we'll use the database to store the valid data and create Java code to query the database to check the results.

Once the servlet validates the user they will be redirected to the home page. If they entered an invalid password they will be redirected back to the login page.

How the Servlet Finds the Next Page

After the servlet has validated and processed all the incoming data, you want to tell it to take the user to the next page.

The last line in your servlet's doPost or doGet methods will handle that. When the servlet comes to this line of code it will send the user to the correct page.

```
//redirect to next page as indicated by the value of the
nextURL variable
String nextURL = "home.jsp";

getServletContext().getRequestDispatcher(nextURL)
    .forward(request,response);
```

How to Set Values on Your Output Page

Create a jsp page called home.jsp. Add the following code to your page so it will read the values of the parameters from the servlet. The notation ${userEmail} will read the parameter from the request packet. You set that in the servlet.

```
<html>
    <head>
        <title>The results of my form</title>
    </head>
<body>
    <h1>Using GET Method to Read Form Data</h1>
```

```
        <ul>
            <li><p><b>First Name:</b> ${firstName} </p></li>
            <li><p><b>Last Name:</b> ${lastName} </p></li>
        </ul>
</body>
</html>
```

How the Log Out Button Works

When the user wants to log out, you simply end their session. That makes logging out easy. Most users won't click the Log Out button. For them, the session ends when the session timeout is reached. You can set the session timeout property or use the default of 20 minutes.

Create a form that will pass a parameter called `action` with a value of `logout` to your login servlet. To pass that parameter, you'll create a hidden input and give it a name and ID of `action` with a value of `logout`.

The form's action will be the name of the login servlet. When the servlet receives the parameter it will invalidate the session and redirect the user to the login page. The Java code to end a session is `session.invalidate();`.

The Login Servlet Code

Listing 9-2. The Code for the Login Servlet

```
//LoginServlet.java
package controller;
/*
 * the login servlet processes login.jsp. The servlet has one
job
```

```
 * which is to validate the user and add them to the session so
 * that user will be available to all pages. If the user is not
   valid
 * then the login servlet will redirect back to the login page.
 */

import java.io.IOException;
import javax.servlet.ServletException;
import javax.servlet.annotation.WebServlet;
import javax.servlet.http.HttpServlet;
import javax.servlet.http.HttpServletRequest;
import javax.servlet.http.HttpServletResponse;
import javax.servlet.http.HttpSession;
import service.DbUser;
import model.Bhuser;

@WebServlet("/LoginServlet")
public class LoginServlet extends HttpServlet {
        private static final long serialVersionUID = 1L;

    public LoginServlet() {
        super();
    }

        protected void doPost(HttpServletRequest request,
        HttpServletResponse response) throws ServletException,
        IOException {
                //this page does not require user to be
                logged in
                String useremail = request.getParameter
                ("email");
                String userpassword = request.getParameter
                ("password");
```

```
String action = request.getParameter("action");
//String remember = request.getParameter
("remember");
String nextURL = "/error.jsp";

//get an instance of the session so we can set
attributes to it
//the JSP and NavBar will read from the session
//The session is one of the primary ways we
maintain state
//in an otherwise stateless web application
HttpSession session = request.getSession();

//create an instance of the user and put it in
the session
//only add the user to the session if the user
if valid.
//The presence of the user is used to determine
who
//owns the site and will be used to connect to
the database
if (action.equals("logout")){
        session.invalidate();
        nextURL = "/login.jsp";

}else{
        if (DbUser.isValidUser(useremail,
        userpassword)){
                Bhuser user = DbUser.
                getUserByEmail(useremail);
                session.setAttribute
                ("user", user);
                int gravatarImageWidth = 30;
```

```
                                String gravatarURL =
                                        DbUser.getGravatarURL
                                        (useremail,
                                        gravatarImageWidth);
                                session.setAttribute
                                ("gravatarURL", gravatarURL);
                                nextURL = "/home.jsp";
                        }else{
                                nextURL = "/login.jsp";
                        }
                }
                //redirect to next page as indicated by the
                value of the nextURL variable
                getServletContext().getRequest
                Dispatcher(nextURL).forward(request,response);
        }

}
//End of LoginServlet.java
```

The News Feed Servlet Code

Listing 9-3. The Code for the News Feed Servlet

```
//Newsfeed.java
package controller;

import java.io.IOException;
import java.util.List;
import javax.servlet.ServletException;
import javax.servlet.annotation.WebServlet;
import javax.servlet.http.HttpServlet;
```

```
import javax.servlet.http.HttpServletRequest;
import javax.servlet.http.HttpServletResponse;
import javax.servlet.http.HttpSession;
import model.Bhpost;
import service.DbPost;

@WebServlet("/Newsfeed")
public class Newsfeed extends HttpServlet {
        private static final long serialVersionUID = 1L;

    public Newsfeed() {
        super();
    }

        protected void doGet(HttpServletRequest request,
        HttpServletResponse response) throws ServletException,
        IOException {
                //users can get to this servlet through a get
                request so handle it here
                //With a get request the parameters are part of
                the url.
                //We already handle everything in doPost so
                just call that.
                doPost(request,response);
        }

        protected void doPost(HttpServletRequest request,
        HttpServletResponse response) throws ServletException,
        IOException {
                long filterByUserID = 0;
                String searchtext = "";

                //set the value of the next page. It should
                change in the code below.
```

```
String nextURL = "/error.jsp";

//get user out of session.
//If they don't exist then send them back to
the login page.
//kill the session while you're at it.
HttpSession session = request.getSession();
if (session.getAttribute("user")==null){
        nextURL = "/login.jsp";
        session.invalidate();
        response.sendRedirect(request.
        getContextPath() + nextURL);
    return;//return prevents an error
}

//get posts based on parameters; if no
parameters then get all posts
List<Bhpost> posts = null;
if (request.getParameter("userid")!=null
                && !request.getParameter
                ("userid").isEmpty()){
        filterByUserID = Integer.parseInt
        (request.getParameter("userid"));
        posts = DbPost.postsofUser
        (filterByUserID);

}else if (request.getParameter("searchtext")!=
null
                && !request.getParameter
                ("searchtext").isEmpty()){
        searchtext = request.getParameter
        ("searchtext").toString();
        posts = DbPost.searchPosts(searchtext);
```

```
            }else{
                    posts = DbPost.bhPost();
            }

            //add posts to request
            request.setAttribute("posts", posts);
            //display posts in newsfeed.jsp
            nextURL = "/newsfeed.jsp";
            //redirect to next page as indicated by the
            value of the nextURL variable
            getServletContext().getRequestDispatcher
            (nextURL).forward(request,response);
    }

}
//end of Newsfeed.java
```

The PostServ Servlet Code

Listing 9-4. The Code for the PostServ Servlet

```
//PostServ.java
package controller;

import java.io.IOException;
import javax.servlet.ServletException;
import javax.servlet.annotation.WebServlet;
import javax.servlet.http.HttpServlet;
import javax.servlet.http.HttpServletRequest;
import javax.servlet.http.HttpServletResponse;
import javax.servlet.http.HttpSession;
import java.util.Calendar;
```

```
import java.util.Date;
import model.Bhpost;
import model.Bhuser;
import service.DbPost;

@WebServlet("/PostServ")
public class PostServ extends HttpServlet {
        private static final long serialVersionUID = 1L;

    public PostServ() {
        super();
    }

    protected void doPost(HttpServletRequest request,
                                    HttpServletResponse
                                    response)
                                          throws
                                          ServletException,
                                          IOException {

            String posttext = request.getParameter
            ("posttext");
            String nextURL = "/error.jsp";

            //Get user out of session. If they don't exist then
            //end the session and send them back to the
            login page.
            HttpSession session = request.getSession();
            if (session.getAttribute("user")==null){
                    nextURL = "/login.jsp";
                    session.invalidate();
            } else {
```

```
            //Get the user out of the session
            Bhuser bhuser = (Bhuser)session.getAttribute
            ("user");

            //insert the post
            Bhpost bhPost = new Bhpost();
            bhPost.setBhuser(bhuser);
            Date postdate = Calendar.getInstance().
            getTime();//today's date
            bhPost.setPostdate(postdate);
            bhPost.setPosttext(posttext);
            DbPost.insert(bhPost);
            nextURL = "/Newsfeed";//go to newsfeed servlet
            to show all posts
            }

            //the value of nextURL will be newsfeed, login,
             or error
            getServletContext().getRequestDispatcher(nextURL)
                .forward(request, response);
        }
}
//end of PostServ.java
```

The Profile Servlet Code

Listing 9-5. The Code for the Profile Servlet

```
//ProfileServlet.java
package controller;
```

```
import java.io.IOException;
import javax.servlet.ServletException;
import javax.servlet.annotation.WebServlet;
import javax.servlet.http.HttpServlet;
import javax.servlet.http.HttpServletRequest;
import javax.servlet.http.HttpServletResponse;
import javax.servlet.http.HttpSession;
import java.text.SimpleDateFormat;
import service.DbUser;
import model.Bhuser;

@WebServlet("/ProfileServlet")
public class ProfileServlet extends HttpServlet {
        private static final long serialVersionUID = 1L;

    public ProfileServlet() {
        super();
    }

    protected void doGet(HttpServletRequest request,
    HttpServletResponse response) throws ServletException,
    IOException {
            doPost(request,response);
    }
        protected void doPost(HttpServletRequest request,
        HttpServletResponse response) throws ServletException,
        IOException {
                /*
                 * simplify this so that it always requires two
                   parameters, userid and action
                 * action is view or edit. If edit then the
                   userID of the session(user) must be same as
                   userID for profile
```

```
 * since you can only edit your own.
 * all urls coming to this page must contain
   both parameters or get error.
 */
HttpSession session = request.getSession();
String nextURL = "/error.jsp";
long userid = 0;
String action = "";
Bhuser profileUser = null;
Bhuser loggedInUser = null;

//get user out of session. If they don't exist
then send them back to the login page.
//kill the session while you're at it.
if (session.getAttribute("user")==null){
        nextURL = "/login.jsp";
        session.invalidate();
        response.sendRedirect(request.
        getContextPath() + nextURL);
    return;//return prevents an error
}

try{
userid = Long.parseLong(request.getParameter
("userid"));
action = request.getParameter("action");

//update profile for user in request variable
if action = updateprofile
if (request.getParameter("action").
equals("updateprofile")){
        long uid = Long.parseLong
        (request.getParameter("userid"));
```

```
                String userEmail = request.getParameter
                ("useremail");
                String userMotto = request.getParameter
                ("usermotto");
                Bhuser updateUser = DbUser.getUser(uid);
                updateUser.setMotto(userMotto);
                updateUser.setUseremail(userEmail);
                DbUser.update(updateUser);
        }

        //get the user from the parameter
        profileUser = DbUser.getUser(userid);
//get the current user out of the session
        loggedInUser = (Bhuser) session.getAttribute
        ("user");

        if (profileUser.getBhuserid()==loggedInUser.get
        Bhuserid()){
                //display profile as form
                //the session variable editProfile is
                used by the JSP to
                //display the profile in edit mode
                session.setAttribute("editProfile",
                true);
        }else{
                //display profile read-only
                //the session variable editProfile is
                used by the JSP to
                //display the profile in read-only mode
                session.setAttribute("editProfile",
                false);
        }
```

```
//populate the data in the attributes
    int imgSize = 120;
    SimpleDateFormat sdf = new SimpleDateFormat
    ("MMM d, yyyy");
    String joindate = sdf.format(profileUser.
    getJoindate());
    request.setAttribute("userid", profileUser.
    getBhuserid());
    request.setAttribute("userimage",
                    DbUser.getGravatarURL
                    (profileUser.getUseremail(),
                    imgSize));
    request.setAttribute("username", profileUser.
    getUsername());
    request.setAttribute("useremail", profileUser.
    getUseremail());
    request.setAttribute("usermotto", profileUser.
    getMotto());
    request.setAttribute("userjoindate", joindate);
    nextURL = "/profile.jsp";

    }catch(Exception e){
            //print the exception so we can see it
            while testing the application
            //in production it isn't a good idea to
            print to the console since it
            //consumes resources and will not be seen
            System.out.println(e);
    }
    //redirect to next page as indicated by the
    value of the nextURL variable
```

```
                getServletContext().getRequestDispatcher
                (nextURL)

        .forward(request,response);
        }
}
//ProfileServlet.java
```

The AddUser Servlet Code

Listing 9-6. The Code for the AddUser Servlet

```
//AddUser.java
package controller;

import java.io.IOException;
import java.util.Calendar;
import java.util.Date;

import javax.servlet.ServletException;
import javax.servlet.annotation.WebServlet;
import javax.servlet.http.HttpServlet;
import javax.servlet.http.HttpServletRequest;
import javax.servlet.http.HttpServletResponse;
import javax.servlet.http.HttpSession;

import model.Bhuser;
import service.DbUser;

@WebServlet("/AddUser")
public class AddUser extends HttpServlet {
        private static final long serialVersionUID = 1L;
    public AddUser() {
```

```
        super();
    }

        protected void doPost(HttpServletRequest request,
                HttpServletResponse response) throws
                ServletException, IOException {

                HttpSession session = request.getSession();

                //This page does not require user to be logged in
                String userName = request.getParameter
                ("userName");
                String userEmail = request.getParameter
                ("userEmail");
                String userPassword = request.getParameter
                ("userPassword");
                String userMotto = request.getParameter
                 ("userMotto");
                String nextURL = "/error.jsp";
                //check if user exists (by email)
                Bhuser user = DbUser.getUserByEmail(userEmail);

                //create user and add them if they don't exit
                if (user == null){
                        user = new Bhuser();
                        user.setUsername(userName);
                        user.setUseremail(userEmail);
                        user.setUserpassword(userPassword);
                        Date joindate = Calendar.getInstance().
                        getTime();
                        user.setJoindate(joindate);
                        user.setMotto(userMotto);
```

```
                    DbUser.insert(user);
                    nextURL = "/home.jsp";
            }else{
                    String message = "You have an
                    account - ";
                    request.setAttribute("message",
                    message);
                    nextURL = "/login.jsp";
            }

            //add the user to the session
            session.setAttribute("user", user);

            //redirect to next page as indicated by the
            value of the nextURL variable
            getServletContext().getRequestDispatcher(nextURL)

        .forward(request,response);
        }

}
// end of AddUser.java
```

CHAPTER 10

The Presentation/View

Users interact with your application through their web browser. The role of the web browser is to display the HTML, JavaScript, and images. Each web document contains a section we call the head and a section we call the body.

The head contains the title tag, link tag, and script tag. The link and script tags allow the page to include external files for style sheets and JavaScript, respectively. Our application will contain links to style sheets and JavaScript for Bootstrap.

The body of the document has more information. The body is where the content seen in the browser will go. This includes the form, text displayed to the user, links, and images. All the content in the body will be marked up with tags, which determine how the content will render.

You can include comments in your web page that won't show to the user. They help you document your page layout.

D. Wolf and A.J. Henley, *Java EE Web Application Primer*,
https://doi.org/10.1007/978-1-4842-3195-1_10

CHAPTER 11

Designing Web Pages with HTML

HTML (hypertext markup language) is a markup language for creating web documents (web pages). The main function of a browser is to receive the web page as HTML from the web server and display it. The browser applies all fonts, styles, and layouts specified by the HTML tags and CSS property values. This content can be further manipulated by using JavaScript, the programming language of the browser.

The document object model (DOM) is a representation of your HTML document as a tree structure. The DOM sees each node as an object representing a part of the document. The objects can be manipulated programmatically by JavaScript, allowing your page to interact with the user.

Here's all you need to know about HTML:

- HTML documents are composed of elements called tags.
- The collection of HTML elements in a web page document is called the DOM (document object model).
- Tags are used to identify document content and structure.
- Tags often contain attributes that provide parameters for the element.

D. Wolf and A.J. Henley, *Java EE Web Application Primer*,
https://doi.org/10.1007/978-1-4842-3195-1_11

- The HTML document, which contains content and tags, is rendered by the browser to display the formatted version of the web page.
- The latest version of HTML is called HTML5.

CHAPTER 12

HTML5 Tags

A tag is created by putting the tag names in angle brackets, like this: `<tag>`. The word in brackets, in this case *tag*, is the tag name. Tags contain an opening tag and a closing tag. An opening tag contains only the tag name in angle brackets. A closing tag precedes the tag name with a forward slash. For example: `<table></table>`. If a tag contains no data, then the opening and closing tags can be combined, as in `<br/>`.

Tags can contain attributes that give further information about them. HTML5 attributes are created using a name-value pair and are usually put alongside the tag name. In this chapter, we'll discuss attributes and then look at some of the tags we'll use for developing Bullhorn.

Name-value pairs are represented by a set of text strings in which `name="value"` and are usually separated by commas, semicolons, or space or newline characters. HTML5 attributes are written inside the element's tag and separated by spaces. See Listing 12-1.

Listing 12-1. An Example Input Tag from an HTML Form

```
<input type="text" id="email"
    name = "email" value="user@domain.com"/>
```

In this code, the attributes are `type`, `id`, `name`, and `value`, and their values are always in quotes following the equal sign. Attributes provide extra information about an element. We now know, for example, the preceding input element is a text box, is identified by the `name`/`id` `email`, and contains a default value of `user@domain.com`. The `id` attribute is a

D. Wolf and A.J. Henley, *Java EE Web Application Primer*,
https://doi.org/10.1007/978-1-4842-3195-1_12

unique identifier for the element. The id is used by CSS and JavaScript. The name attribute specifies a name for an element. We use the name when retrieving the element's value in the servlet. Use name attributes for form controls (such as <input>). Name is the identifier used in the POST or GET call that happens on form submission. Use the id attribute to identify a particular HTML element with CSS of JavaScript. It's possible to look up elements by name but simpler to use id.

Explanation of Common Tags

- <!DOCTYPE html> Identifies the document as an HTML5 document. This makes sure the document will be parsed the same way by different browsers.
- <head></head> All data in the head section of an HTML document is considered metadata, meaning data about data. The information in this section is not normally displayed directly. Instead, elements such as style affect the appearance of other elements in the document. Some items in the head section may be used by programs such as search engines to learn more about the page for reference purposes.
- <title></title> Belongs in the head section of the document and sets the title that is displayed in the browser tab.
- <body></body> The entire document body is contained within these two tags.
- <h1></h1> Any text contained within these tags is often displayed as a large bold font heading, but the actual formatting is up to the browser. There are six heading tags, h1 (largest) to h6 (smallest).

- <p></p> Any content with the paragraph tags is considered a paragraph. You can add an attribute such as style to the paragraph tags to control which styles impact the text within the paragraph tags.
- <img></img> The image tag is used to display images. It has two attributes you need to use: `src` and `alt`. The `src` attribute contains the path to the image file. The path can be either a filename or a URL. The `alt` attribute contains the alternate text to be displayed when the images don't show or can't be seen. It is also used by screen readers to describe the image. A complete image tag would look like this: `<img src="path/to/filename.png" alt="Picture of my cat"/>`

An HTML form allows the user to submit data to the web server. The data from the form will be sent in the request packet to the servlet. The servlet will receive the data and can use it to either query the database or choose another page to send the user to. See Listing 12-2. Notice that every tag has a closing tag (or contains /> to indicate it is self-closing).

Listing 12-2. Example HTML Form

```
<form action="PostServ" method="post">
<label for="posttext">Create New Post (141 char):</label>
<textarea name="posttext" id="posttext" rows="2"
maxlength="141"></textarea>
<input type="submit" value="Submit" id="submit"/>
<input type="reset" value="Clear"/>
</form>
```

- `<form></form>` The `form` tag contains all the elements of a user input form that gets data from the user and sends it to the servlet. The `form` tag contains two required attributes, `method` and `action`. The `method` attribute can be either `"get"` or `"post"`, and it determines how the data is sent to the servlet. The `action` attribute contains the URL of the servlet that processes the form data.
- `<input></input>` The purpose of a form is to get input from the user and display data that will be sent to the server. The way you get input from the user is with the `input` tag. It will create a text box on the web page. The contents of the `input` tag will be sent to the servlet when the Submit button is clicked. Submit itself is an input. An `input` tag becomes a Submit button when the `type` attribute is set to `"submit"`.

Some example input tags:

- `<input id="email" name="email" type="text" value=""/>` An input tag that displays as a text box and collects the email address of the user
- `<input type="submit" value="Submit" id="submit"/>` An input tag that displays as a button and calls the form's action when clicked
- `<input type="reset" value="Clear"/>` An input tag that displays as a button with a label that says Clear and causes all the form's input boxes to clear
- `<textarea></textarea>` An input that contains multiple rows:`<textarea name="posttext" id="posttext" rows="2" maxlength="141"> </textarea>`

HTML Tables

A table starts with <table> and ends with </table>.

Each table is made of table rows, which start with <tr> and end with </tr>.

Each row is made up of cells of table data, which start with <td> and end with </td>.

The first row of a table can be used as the header row. In this case, change the <td> tags to <th> for the first row. You can change the style of the header row to make it appear different from the other table rows.

<caption>...</caption> is useful for defining or describing the content of the table. Captions are optional. To add a caption to a table, add the caption element after the opening table tag, with the text of the caption inside the element. Captions are usually displayed outside the border of the table, at the top. The exact appearance and placement of captions is subject to CSS styling. See Listing 12-3 and Figure 12-1.

Listing 12-3. Minimal HTML Table Example

```
<table border="1">
    <caption>Formulas and Results</caption>
    <tr><th>Formula</th><th>Result</th></tr>
    <tr><td>1 + 1</td><td>2</td></tr>
    <tr><td>3 * 5</td><td>15</td></tr>
</table>
```

Formulas and Results

Formula	Result
1 + 1	2
3 * 5	15

Figure 12-1. *The table generated from the preceding code*

A Basic HTML5 and JSP Document

A JSP (JavaServer Pages) page is a dynamic HTML page. It contains both HTML and JSP tags. The content can change depending on the data the user is viewing.

A JSP is still a text document. It also contains HTML tags just like an HTML document. But there's more. The JSP can receive and display data sent by the servlet. Now you can personalize your site for each user, whereas an HTML page displays the same for every user. JSTL allows you to embed logic within a JSP page without using Java code directly. Using standardized tags is not only more secure, but it also allows code to be more maintainable and keeps the Java code separate from the user interface. This template would be saved as a text document with a .jsp extension. See Listing 12-4.

Listing 12-4. The Structure of a Basic HTML/JSP Page

```
<%@ page language="java" contentType="text/html; charset=UTF-8"
pageEncoding="UTF-8"%>
<%@ taglib prefix="c"
    uri="http://java.sun.com/jsp/jstl/core" %>
<%@ taglib prefix="fmt"
    uri="http://java.sun.com/jsp/jstl/fmt" %>
<!DOCTYPE html>
<html>
<head>
<meta http-equiv="Content-Type" content="text/html; UTF-8">
<title>Insert title here</title>
</head>
<body>
<h1>This is a sample heading</h1>
```

```
<h2>This is a sub heading</h2>
<p>This is paragraph text</p>
<img src="imagefile.jpg" alt="image description"/>
</body>
</html>
```

JSP Standard Tag Library (JSTL)

The JSP Standard Tag Library (JSTL) is a collection of useful tags you can add to your JSP pages. These tags add functionality common to many JSP applications. JSTL adds support for common structural tasks, such as iteration and conditionals. They also add support for properly escaping HTML or XML code in your pages. This prevents the tags from being evaluated and potentially executing malicious code.

EL (expression language) is a subset of JSTL that makes it easy to use Java classes (called beans) in your JSP. Expression language has a compact syntax and allows you to access the nested properties of objects. For example, a `post` object contains a user. Expression language allows your JSP to access the `getUsername()` method of the user with the relaxed syntax of `${user.username}`. Expression language can also retrieve the values of scalar variables set from the servlet using syntax such as `${message}`.

To include JSTL in your JSP, add the directives shown in the following code listing (Listing 12-5) to the top of your page. Exact placement isn't important, but just above the `<html>` tag is a good place. JSTL is composed of libraries that add functionality for tasks such as looping and if/else statements, as well as formatting numbers, dates, and times. Since we know we want to include looping and if/else functionality in our JSP, and we want to also format dates, we'll include both the core library and the formatting library. See Listing 12-5.

Listing 12-5. JSTL Directives Which Should Be Included Just Above the <HTML> Tag on Your Page. The C Prefix Includes Tags from the Core Library. The FMT Prefix Includes Tags from the Formatting Library.

```
<%@ taglib prefix="c" uri="http://java.sun.com/jsp/jstl/core" %>
<%@ taglib prefix="fmt" uri="http://java.sun.com/jsp/jstl/fmt" %>
```

HOW TO USE JSTL TAGS IN YOUR JSP

1. Copy the following two Java archive (jar) files from the files included with this book to the `WEB-INF/lib` folder of a dynamic web application.

    i. `taglibs-standard-impl-1.2.5.jar`

    ii. `javax.servlet.jsp.jstl-api-1.2.1.jar`

2. Add the following directives to include the core and formatting libraries for JSTL to the top of the page:

    ```
    <%@ taglib prefix="c" uri="http://java.sun.
    com/jsp/jstl/core" %>

    <%@ taglib prefix="fmt" uri="http://java.
    sun.com/jsp/jstl/fmt" %>
    ```

You can now use any of the JSTL tags discussed next.

What Can You Do with JSTL?

Prevent Cross-site Scripting Attacks

Cross-site scripting (XSS) is a computer security vulnerability that occurs when malicious users input scripts or other code into your website through the text boxes on your web pages. The JSTL `core out` tag prevents cross-site scripting attacks. The `c:out` escapes any input from the user so it is no longer executable. If a user entered malicious JavaScript in a text box on your website, that JavaScript would be executed and could compromise the data. The `c:out` JSTL tag reduces this vulnerability.

Loop Through a Collection

The JSTL `forEach` tag provides a mechanism to loop through the items in a collection. The collection can be set in the servlet, and the JSTL code in your JSP will loop through it and repeat the code between the `forEach` open and closing tags. Any HTML in between those tags will also be repeated for each item in the collection. You can see an example of the `forEach` tag in the `newsfeed.jsp` page. See also Listing 12-6.

Listing 12-6. The JSTL forEach Tag Allows You to Loop Through a Collection of Posts

```
<c:forEach var="post" items="${posts}">
    <c:out value="${post.user.username}"/><br/>
    <c:out value="${post.posttext}"/>
</c:forEach>
```

Set a Value

The code in Listing 12-7 shows how to set the value of a variable called `number`. You can then refer to the variable later in the page or even the session. To refer to the variable only on the current page, set the scope to `"request"`. To refer to the variable on other pages in your application, set the scope to `"session"`, which applies just to a single user, or `"application"`, which applies to all users. You can then use the variable with a `c:out` tag later in your page or application. In the example here we simply set the value to some random value, say, 10.

Listing 12-7. Using the set Tag of the JSTL Core Library

```
<c:set var="number" scope="session" value="10"/>
<c:out value="${number}"/>
```

Test a Condition

JSTL allows you to include or exclude code based on a condition. In the example in Listing 12-8, the value of the variable called `number` determines if the content between the JSTL `if` tags will be displayed or not.

Listing 12-8. JSTL Allows You to Show or Hide Code Based on a Condition

```
<c:set var="number" scope="session" value="10"/>

<c:if test="${number<100}">
<c:out value=
   "this line will print if number is less than 100">
</c:out>
<p>Any content between the if tags will
   display when the condition if true</p>
</c:if>
```

Repeat Content a Fixed Number of Times

The JSTL core library `forEach` tag will repeat content a fixed number of times. The content is whatever you have specified in between the opening and closing `forEach` tags. The content will be repeated the number of times indicated by the `begin` and `end` attributes, inclusively. In the code in Listing 12-9, the numbers 5 6 7 8 9 10 will be displayed in the browser.

Listing 12-9. JSTL Allows You to Repeat Content a Fixed Number of Times

```
<c:forEach var="number" begin="5" end="10">
    <c:out value="${number}"></c:out>
</c:forEach>
```

Test a Condition and Choose an Alternative

JSTL does not feature an `else` clause to go with the `if` statement. However, the JSTL core `when` and `otherwise` tags work like an if-else statement when placed inside the JSTL core `choose` tag. You can have any number of `when` tags but only one `otherwise` tag. See Listing 12-10.

Listing 12-10. The JSTL choose, when, and otherwise Tags Allow You to Simulate an if/else Condition

```
<c:choose>
        <c:when test="${number % 2==0}">
         <p>
        <c:out value="The number is an even number">
        </c:out>
        </p>
        </c:when>
        <c:otherwise>
         <p>
```

```
        <c:out value="The number is an odd number">
        </c:out></p>
        </c:otherwise>
</c:choose>
```

Determine If a String Is Null or Empty

JSTL will allow your code to test a value and determine if the value is null or empty. As shown in the code in Listing 12-11, you pass the variable, which can be set in the servlet or from a collection you're looping through. Then, if the string is null or empty, the code between the `c:if` statements will execute. If HTML code is between the `c:if` tags then it will be displayed in the browser when the condition is true. You can negate the condition by placing the word `not` prior to the word `empty`.

Listing 12-11. Test If a Variable Is Null or Empty

```
<c:if test="${empty var1}">
<h2>var1 is empty or null.</h2>
</c:if>
```

Formatting Dates

JSTL will allow you to display dates in a format you specify. We use this in Bullhorn when we display the post date. We only want to see the date as the year followed by the month abbreviation and then the day. The value of the date should be a `Date` object, `java.util.Date`. If your date is a `String` object, then you should convert it first. The JSTL `formatDate` tag will format a date according to the specified pattern. See Listing 12-12.

Listing 12-12. Using the JSTL Format Library to Format a Date

```
<fmt:formatDate value="${post.postdate}"
     pattern="yy-MMM-dd"/>
```

How to Display Form Data

Java web applications typically contain forms that collect user input and pass it to a servlet for processing. The servlet can then communicate with the database and do something with the data. Once the servlet is finished working with the data it will send a new web page to the browser with the results of the form. All this happens in an instant on the server and out of the sight of the user.

Create an HTML Login Form

HTML forms allow users to submit data to your servlet.

We want to enable the user to log in with their email and a password. So, we need to create a web page with an HTML login form.

The form should contain two text boxes—one for username and one for password. The form needs a Submit button. The text boxes and button must be contained within the tags that declare the form so they will be submitted to the URL of the login servlet indicated in the `action` attribute of the `form` tag.

All attribute values must be in quotes and in the format of `attribute="value"`. These values will be used by the web server to determine how the form is processed.

The form will not work until we create the servlet. The servlet is a container that can run Java code and process our form. It will receive the values from the inputs. Then, we can write Java code to do something with the inputs.

```
<!DOCTYPE html>
<html>
<body>
    <h1>Login</h1>
    <!--the action will be set to the same value as
```

```
    the servlet's @WebServlet annotation -->
    <form action="LoginServlet" method="post">
        Email Address:<br>
        <input type="text" name="email"><br>
        Password:<br>
        <input type="password" name="password"><br><br>

        <input type="submit" value="Submit">
    </form>
</body>
</html>
```

The resulting web form can be seen in Figure 12-2.

Login

Email Address:

Password:

Submit

Figure 12-2. *If you click the Submit button, the form's data will be sent to a servlet called LoginServlet.java, which contains an @WebServlet annotation at the top of the code set to 'loginServlet'.*

Be sure to set the `action` attribute of your form to match your servlet's @WebServlet annotation.

Create a Page to Display the Output of Your Form

Next, we will create a JSP to display the output of the form. The form will send its data to the servlet, and the servlet will send the data to the output JSP. While it's possible to bypass the servlet, there's no good reason to do so since any application of significance will use the servlet to perform some processing. The page to display the output will be called, simply enough, `output.jsp`. See Listing 12-13. The page will not display anything since there is not HTML code in the body.

Listing 12-13. A Simple JSP Page, output.jsp

```
<%@ page language="java"
        contentType="text/html;
        charset=UTF-8"
        pageEncoding="UTF-8"%>
<!DOCTYPE html
        PUBLIC "-//W3C//DTD HTML 4.01 Transitional//EN"
        "http://www.w3.org/TR/html4/loose.dtd">

<html>
<head>
<meta http-equiv="Content-Type"
        content="text/html; charset=UTF-8">
Page
</head>
<body>

</body>
</html>
```

How to Allow the User to Navigate Between Web Pages

Links are found in nearly all web pages. Links allow users to click their way from page to page. HTML links are called *hyperlinks*. They are defined with the `<a>` tag:

```
<a href="_url_">_link text_</a>
```

A hyperlink is text or an image you can click on to jump to another document. For example:

```
<a href="http://www.somesite.com/">Visit Some Site</a>
```

A local link (link to the same website) is specified with a relative URL (without `http://www.`...):

```
<a href="index2.html">My other page</a>
```

Reusing JSP Code

Writing code is fun. Writing the same code repetitively is . . . repetitive. And not fun. Java Server Pages allow you to reuse code by creating include files. An include file is simply a JSP or fragment of a JSP (or HTML) that you include in your existing page. The advantage of including some fragment of code in one page is that you can then include that same fragment in other pages, saving you valuable time from rewriting the same code. The code for the navigation bar for Bullhorn goes at the top of every page, just below the opening body tag. I *could* copy that code to every page. Then, if I choose to modify it, I *could* open every page and modify every page. A better idea is to put the code for the navigation bar in one JSP file and add an `include` tag at the location where I want the navigation bar to appear (see Listings 12-14 to 12-16). Now I only need to change or update the navigation bar in one place. Nice!

Listing 12-14. The include Directive That Goes in Every Page to Include the navbar on Bullhorn

```
<jsp:include page="navbar.jsp"></jsp:include>
```

Listing 12-15. The First Two Lines of navbar.jsp (you can view the entire file in the source code that accompanies this book)

```
<nav class="navbar navbar-default">
  <div class="container-fluid">
```

Listing 12-16. The Last Three Lines of navbar.jsp (you can view the entire file in the source code that accompanies this book)

```
      </ul>
    </div><!-- /.navbar-collapse -->
  </div><!-- /.container-fluid -->
</nav>
```

Customizing Your Errors

While you are developing your application, you probably won't want to implement custom error pages. The Tomcat error pages are exactly what you need, with all the information you could want in one place.

Once you are ready to deploy your application, the default error pages lack . . . polish . . . and can be a sign of an unprofessional application.

There are two kinds of errors that you are going to want your application to be able to handle: HTML errors and Java exceptions.

The main HTML errors you need to handle are the 404 error (page not found) and the 500 error (server error).

As for Java exceptions, we can build a general page that handles them all.

HOW TO ADD A CUSTOM ERROR PAGE

The easiest way to handle custom errors is to add entries to the web.xml file. By default, the web.xml file is not available, so to add it you need to do the following:

1. Right-click your dynamic web project.
2. Select Java EE Tools ➤ Generate Deployment Descriptor Stub.
3. Double-click the web.xml file in WebContent/WEB-INF.
4. Add an extra line before </web-app> and insert the following:

```
<error-page>
    <error-code>404</error-code>
    <location>/error_404.jsp</location>
</error-page>
```

5. Then, create a corresponding JSP with the proper message.

If you run your application and try to navigate to a page that doesn't exist, you should now get your new custom error page.

To create your own attractive page for handling ALL Java exceptions, add the following to your web.xml file:

```
<error-page>
   <location>/error_java.jsp</location>
</error-page>
```

Then, put something like the following in your error_java.jsp:

```
<h1>Error</h1>
<p>Sorry, Java has thrown an exception.</p>
<p>To continue, click the Back button.</p>

<h2>Details</h2>
<p>Type: ${pageContext.exception["class"]}</p>
<p>Message: ${pageContext.exception.message}</p>
```

CHAPTER 13

The Stateless Nature of the Web

A web application does not maintain state. It has no memory. Each request to the web server is an independent event. Each request does not know about previous requests. When you send your username and password, the web server views this as an independent event. It does not keep track of what you're logging in to. The information is simply sent to the server.

When you submit a form, all the information about what to do with the form data must be sent along with the form. Why? Because each request is an independent transaction.

In real life this is what it would be like if you went to the bank and got a new teller after each question. And the tellers don't talk to each other—only to you. And each teller would want to see your ID and check your balance and do everything the other teller had already done. To make such a situation easier, you could keep a running log of each transaction that each teller could use to verify what has been done.

So, how does a web application maintain state? The answer is by using either session variables or passing information known as parameters from the previous transaction. Parameters are sent between the client (web browser) and the server via either the URL or as other information sent to the server as part of the request. This is called the request packet; we have touched on this already in our discussion of servlets.

D. Wolf and A.J. Henley, *Java EE Web Application Primer*,
https://doi.org/10.1007/978-1-4842-3195-1_13

Session variables exist in the memory of the web server. Each request includes a session ID. The session ID links the request to the session data for that user. The session ID is automatically passed between requests. You don't have to do anything. It's always there.

Since there is one session per user, you can store variables in each user's session. This is a space in memory that holds data while the user is using the site. Since Java always knows the session ID, it has access to any data in the session.

So, it's the request packet and the session that tie the room together. And you thought it was the rug! (Not funny? Watch *The Big Lebowski* again). A session makes it easy for the server to connect one request to another.

The Process of Passing Data

The following list is a summary of the steps that are followed for data to be sent from a web form to a JSP using a servlet:

1. The form passes the request.
2. Servlet receives the request.
3. The servlet processes the request with `request.getParameter()`.
4. The servlet generates a response based on the data in the request.
5. The servlet constructs a response in an object that will be sent to the JSP.
6. The JSP contains an attribute `${user}`.

7. The servlet sets the attribute `request.setAttribute ("user",myUser);`.

8. The servlet sends the JSP back to the originating browser by calling `getServletContext(). getRequestDispatcher(url).forward(request, response);`.

CHAPTER 14

Users and Sessions

The user first accesses your site through the login page. The user's email and password are validated against the database in the login servlet. A user email with the correct matching password is presumed to be a valid user. The valid user is retrieved from the database and stored in the User object. Recall that the User object is generated by the "JPA Generate Entities from Tables" option.

A User object that is stored in the session is easily available to every servlet or JSP in your site. The login servlet validated the user and sent them to the next page, but the next page doesn't know anything about the user. We put the user in the session, and the next page, as well as other pages in our application, can access the session and therefore the user. See Listing 14-1.

Listing 14-1. The Private Member Variables of the User Class Correspond with the User Table

```
@Entity
@NamedQuery(name="Bhuser.findAll",
        query="SELECT b FROM Bhuser b")
public class Bhuser
                implements Serializable {
        @Id
        @GeneratedValue(
                strategy=GenerationType.IDENTITY)
```


D. Wolf and A.J. Henley, *Java EE Web Application Primer*,
https://doi.org/10.1007/978-1-4842-3195-1_14

```
        private long bhuserid;
        @Temporal(TemporalType.DATE)
        private Date joindate;
        private String motto;
        private String useremail;
        private String username;
        private String userpassword;
```

Each user can create many posts. Each post in the database contains the user ID pointing back to the user. The user table keeps track of the posts by placing all the posts in a list. Therefore, the User object contains a list of all the posts for that user, not just the PostId. See Listing 14-2.

Listing 14-2. The Private Member Variable for the Posts Corresponds to the Posts Table. The User Contains Posts So the Posts Are Implemented as a List.

```
@OneToMany(mappedBy="bhuser")
private List<Bhpost> bhposts;
```

The user class is a POJO—Plain Old Java Object. It contains getters and setters for each private member variable. The getter and setter for the user ID are shown in Listing 14-3. The naming convention is: always the word get or set followed by the capitalized private member variable name. You'll see later when we are accessing the variable in the JSP pages that the word get or set can be eliminated and the JSP will still find the correct value. You don't have to program this behavior—it's part of the Java Standard Tag Library.

Listing 14-3. Getter and Setter for the User Class

```
public long getBhuserid() {
        return this.bhuserid;
}
```

```
public void setBhuserid(long bhuserid) {
        this.bhuserid = bhuserid;
}
```

The session allows every page to display the user's name, email, and Gravatar. Java servlets provide a variable called `HttpSession` that we use to identify a user across multiple page requests. Sessions persist for twenty minutes (by default) after they are last used.

Your program obtains a reference to the `HttpSession` object by calling the `getSession()` method of `HttpServletRequest`. The request is stored in a variable called `request` and is managed by Tomcat, the servlet container. See Listing 14-4.

Listing 14-4. By Adding This line of Code, Any Servlet in the Application Can Access Objects Stored in the Session.

```
javax.servlet.http.HttpSession session =
    request.getSession();
```

Think of a session as the memory common to all your application's servlets and JSPs. It works like the Windows clipboard. One servlet puts data into the session, and another JSP can access a copy of it.

Adding Objects to the Session

Objects stored in the session can be accessed by different pages in the application. Add objects to the session in the login servlet as soon as you validate the user. The object is then available for use on other pages of the application. See Listing 14-5.

Listing 14-5. Adding a User to the Session. This Code Can Be Found in the Login Servlet

```
User user = new User();
user.setUserName("Larry");
user.setEmail("larry12345@domain.com");
//add the user to the session
session.setAttribute("user", user);
```

To Read a Value from the Session

The user is stored in the session as an object. When you retrieve the user from the session, you need to cast it to the `User` object and assign it to a variable so you can work with it. See Listing 14-6.

Listing 14-6. Retrieving a Value from the Session

```
User user = (User) session.getAttribute("user");
//now we can get values out of the class
String username = user.getUserName();
String email = user.getEmail();
```

CHAPTER 15

How to Create Database Tables for Bullhorn

Scripts for creating the database tables are included with the source code for Bullhorn. I usually recommend saving SQL scripts in a folder within your project called SQL Scripts so you can easily recreate the database on other systems.

To create a table in a database, you code the table name followed by the field names and data types, as shown in Listing 15-1. The POSTID and BHUSERID fields in the code listing are generated by the database.

You can create the tables by running the scripts found in the SQL Scripts folder of Bullhorn. Copy the code to SQL Developer and press F5 to run the scripts.

Listing 15-1. Code for Creating BHPOST and BHUSER Tables

```
CREATE TABLE BHPOST
 (    POSTID NUMBER
        GENERATED BY DEFAULT ON NULL AS IDENTITY,
      POSTDATE DATE DEFAULT NULL,
      POSTTEXT VARCHAR2(141 BYTE) DEFAULT NULL,
      BHUSERID NUMBER DEFAULT NULL
 ) ;
```


D. Wolf and A.J. Henley, *Java EE Web Application Primer*,
https://doi.org/10.1007/978-1-4842-3195-1_15

```
CREATE TABLE BHUSER
 (      BHUSERID NUMBER
        GENERATED BY DEFAULT ON NULL AS IDENTITY,
        USERNAME VARCHAR2(50 BYTE),
        USERPASSWORD VARCHAR2(50 BYTE),
        MOTTO VARCHAR2(100 BYTE) DEFAULT NULL,
        USEREMAIL VARCHAR2(100 BYTE),
        JOINDATE DATE DEFAULT NULL
 );
```

CHAPTER 16

Make Web Pages Do Something Using JavaScript

JavaScript is the language of the browser. It is an object-oriented programming language. Although JavaScript looks much like Java (because both were based on C and C++), it is not at all related. JavaScript is often used to programmatically interact with an HTML page. It does this by interacting with the DOM (document object model. JavaScript is supported by all major browsers).

Include JavaScript in your web page by putting the script between `<script>` and `</script>` tags. You can place the script tags in the head section or at the bottom of page. If you place the JavaScript on top of your page or between the `<head>` tags, the user may see a blank page for a few seconds. However, once the page is loaded, everything will be fully functional from the first second. If you place the JavaScript at the bottom of the page, the page will seem to load faster, but the JavaScript will not run until the page (and script) is fully loaded. JavaScript may also be saved in a text file (no script tags are needed in this case) and referenced in the head section of your page. This allows you to reuse the same JavaScript on multiple pages. Using linked files is better from a maintenance perspective since all the JavaScript resides in only one location, making updates easy.

D. Wolf and A.J. Henley, *Java EE Web Application Primer*,
https://doi.org/10.1007/978-1-4842-3195-1_16

Because many developers find JavaScript challenging to work with, various libraries have been developed over the years to simplify the routine tasks of working with JavaScript. JQuery (`http://www.jquery.com`) works across all browsers that support JavaScript and makes working with JavaScript much more consistent. JQuery is used extensively in BootStrap. We will look at BootStrap shortly; it makes working with JQuery, HTML, and CSS even more fun.

Note Manipulating the DOM is one of JavaScript's more powerful uses. With DOM, you can navigate through and modify an entire page, ranging from simply adding an element to rearranging several areas on the page. DOM breaks up a document into a *tree* of *nodes*.

Validate a Form Using JavaScript

The form in Listing 16-1 is used to submit a post to Bullhorn. The post should be validated before the user attempts to submit it. JavaScript allows us to do this at the browser. The JavaScript method to validate the form is shown in the listing and contains one method, `validate()`. The JavaScript should be placed between `<script>...</script>` tags at the bottom of the page just before the closing body tag, `</body>`. Placing the script after the elements it references ensures the elements have been created by the DOM before the script is executed. The `validate` method looks at the element with an ID of `posttext` and returns false if the length of this text box is 0 (empty post). A false return will prevent the form from being submitted.

Listing 16-1. A JavaScript Function to Validate the Form Can Go Between Script Tags at the Bottom of the Web Page, Just Before the Closing Body Tag

```
function validate() {
        valid = true;
        if ($('#posttext').val().length==0){
        alert("You may not submit an empty post.");
        valid = false;
        }
return valid;
}
```

The HTML form that will use the preceding validation script goes on your web page within the `<body>...</body>` tags and before your JavaScript. This form will call the script when the Submit button is clicked. If the `validate` method returns false then the form will not be submitted. See Listing 16-2. The `onsubmit` attribute of the `form` tag calls the JavaScript function to validate the form.

Listing 16-2. Form for Submitting a Post

```
<form role="form"
                action="PostServ" method="post"
onsubmit="return validate();">
<label for="post">Create New Post (141 char):</label>
<textarea name="posttext" id="posttext"
                Maxlength="141"></textarea>

<div id="textarea_feedback"></div>


<input type="submit" value="Submit" id="submit"/>
<input type="reset" value="Clear"/>
</form>
```

Display Number of Characters in Text Box

We can also use JavaScript to count the number of characters remaining and update the web page dynamically as the user types. This is an excellent example of the power of JavaScript. It shows that it can be used to manipulate the web page at the browser. This JavaScript function will load when the document is ready. The document is ready after it has been fully rendered and all the DOM has been downloaded from the web server to the browser. Then the function will be created. This function will set the HTML property of the element with the ID of `textarea_feedback` to "XX characters remaining," where XX is the number of remaining characters from the max length of 141. Within `document.ready`, the `keyup` event of the element with an ID of `posttext` is modified to include another function that counts the number of remaining characters and displays them in the `textarea_feedback` element. See Listing 16-3.

Listing 16-3. JavaScript to Return the Number of Characters Remaining in the Text Box

```
$(document).ready(function() {
var text_max = 141;
$('#textarea_feedback').html
     (text_max + ' characters remaining');
  $('#posttext').keyup(function() {
  var text_length = $('#posttext').val().length;

    var text_remaining = text_max - text_length;
      $('#textarea_feedback').html(text_remaining + '
        characters remaining');
    });
});
```

CHAPTER 17

Cascading Style Sheets (CSS)

Cascading Style Sheets (CSS) allow you to specify the visual style and presentation your web application. CSS allows you to separate the style from the structure. This means you are looking through less code when working with your page. The separation of style from structure and content also increases maintainability. Cascading Style Sheets are a set of programmable rules to define how your web pages display content. The styles described by CSS include the colors, fonts, layout, and other presentation aspects of a document, including variations in display for different devices and screen sizes. A single CSS file can describe a common style applicable to many documents.

Typically, an element in an HTML file has a "cascade" of CSS style rules that can be applied to it. The styles cascade based on the location of the definition. If you define a style in multiple locations, then the last definition is applied. You can place your CSS between the `<head>...</head>` tags of a document, in an external style sheet (on your server or on another server), or as a style attribute of an element on your page.

An external style sheet is generally recommended. To link an external style sheet to your document, add a link to the style sheet between the `<head>...</head>` tags of the document. Keeping the style definitions separate from your HTML content minimizes duplication and makes your site easier to maintain.

D. Wolf and A.J. Henley, *Java EE Web Application Primer*,
https://doi.org/10.1007/978-1-4842-3195-1_17

When you create a style sheet, you create a rule for each element by name, class, or ID. These values are set as attributes of the element. The browser will apply the CSS rule when the page is rendered. Each rule has two parts: a selector and a group of one or more declarations surrounded by braces. Each declaration consists of a property name and value pair. There can be several declarations in one rule. See Listing 17-1, which shows an example CSS rule to be applied to all span tags for a document. This rule can be placed in the head section of your web page between `<style>...</style>` tags or in a separate file.

Listing 17-1. Example CSS Rule

```
span {
font-weight: bold;
color: yellow;
background-color: black;
}
```

If you wish to include your CSS rules in a separate file, just add a link to that file in the head section of your web page. See Listing 17-2.

Listing 17-2. Example Link to a Style Sheet

```
<link href="styles/bullhorn.css" rel="stylesheet">
```

Span and Div Tags

Span and div are container tags that define parts of your document. Use span and div to apply styles to a section of a JSP or HTML page. Your page is more organized when you divide it into parts such as header, body, and footer.

The `<div>` tag is used to divide your HTML page into sections and therefore encapsulates various elements. The `<span>` tag is used to group inline elements in a document. The `<div>` and `<span>` tags provide no visual change on their own. These tags provide a way to control the style of part of your document when each tag includes a style, class, or ID attribute. The difference between an ID and a class is that an ID can be used to identify one element while a class can be used to identify multiple elements. When you wish to apply a style to multiple elements, specify the style as a class, since only one element can have an ID attribute with a particular value, but many elements can share the same value in their class attribute. The `<span>` and `<div>` tags have no *required* attributes. The most common attributes used are:

- **style** specifies a style that applies to all content and elements up to the corresponding end tag.
- **class** specifies a CSS class that applies to all content and elements up to the end tag. The value of the class attribute is a CSS class specified in the style sheet file. In the style sheet, the class name is preceded by a period.
- **id** identifies the tag so you can select it with jQuery or JavaScript. The `id` attribute for any element must be unique. In the style sheet, the ID name is preceded by a # hash character.

Listing 17-3. Example HTML Code to Which Styles from Your Style Sheet Will Be Applied

```
<span class="highlight">
<p>This text will be highlighted</p>
</span>
<p name="intro">This text will be red</p>
```

Listing 17-4. Example style sheet that can be placed either between <style> tags in the head section of your JSP page or in a separate file with the link placed within the head section

```
.highlight {
    background-color: yellow;
}
#intro {
  color: red;
}
```

CHAPTER 18

Making Pages Work on All Screen Sizes

Responsive web design (RWD) refers to the approach of developing a web application such that it displays well on any size screen, from desktop computer to mobile phone. A computer, phone, or tablet screen is composed of pixels. A popular screen resolution for a computer is 1366 × 768. That means the screen is 1366 pixels wide and 768 pixels high. Screen resolution determines the clarity with which text and images are displayed. Items appear sharper at higher resolutions. They also appear smaller, which enables more items to fit on screen. When viewed on a tablet the screen may only have 1024 pixels across. A phone has maybe 480 pixels across. Creating a web page so that it displays nicely on different devices is known as making your web page responsive. In the past, developers actually created multiple websites for different devices.

BootStrap (`http://getbootstrap.com`) is a library for developing responsive web applications. It allows you to quickly develop an application interface without spending lots of time learning HTML, CSS, or JavaScript. BootStrap requires jQuery to function. You can implement BootStrap by adding the following to your project:

BootStrap makes its code available via a content delivery network (CDN). That means the latest version of BootStrap is stored on servers scattered around the world. Your page can retrieve the latest version by including a link to the BootStrap CDN in the `HEAD` section of your page.

D. Wolf and A.J. Henley, *Java EE Web Application Primer*,
https://doi.org/10.1007/978-1-4842-3195-1_18

Working with BootStrap

Developers like yourself create code. Designers make the interface look nice. But not every project has a designer. Sometimes that job is also yours. Congratulations!

You have a secret weapon. BootStrap is the most popular HTML, CSS, and JS framework for developing responsive mobile-first projects on the web. BootStrap is a library. It uses HTML, CSS, and JavaScript. It contains design templates for typography, forms, buttons, navigation, and other interface components.

BootStrap allows you to create responsive web pages. Responsive web pages adapt their layout to different devices. Without responsive design, you would have to develop different pages for different devices. BootStrap solves that problem and ends the madness. It is based on a 1170-pixel-wide, 12-column layout. You can set attributes for different devices (and resolutions) in your HTML tags. Listing 18-1 shows an example of a three-column layout that would go in the body of your page. You can easily add additional columns using `div` tags. Place your content in the `body` element.

Listing 18-1. BootStrap Starter Template

```
<!DOCTYPE html>
<html lang="en">
  <head>
    <meta charset="utf-8"/>
    <meta name="viewport"
        content="width=device-width,
        initial-scale=1, shrink-to-fit=no">

    <!-- Bootstrap CSS -->
    <link rel="stylesheet" href=
```

```
"https://maxcdn.bootstrapcdn.com/
        bootstrap/4.0.0-beta/css/bootstrap.min.css">
  </head>
  <body>
    <h1>Hello, world!</h1>

    <script src=
https://code.jquery.com/jquery-3.2.1.slim.min.js/>
    <script src=
"https://cdnjs.cloudflare.com/ajax/libs/popper.js/1.11.0/umd/
popper.min.js">
</script>
    <script src=
"https://maxcdn.bootstrapcdn.com/bootstrap/4.0.0-beta/js/
bootstrap.min.js">
</script>

  </body>
</html>
```

CHAPTER 19

Use Gravatar to Display User's Avatars with Posts

An avatar is an image people use for their online identity. Gravatar is a free service for providing globally unique avatars. Gravatar allows users to register an account using their email address. Users then upload an image to be associated with their Gravatar account. When the user uses the same email address on a website that uses Gravatar, the website retrieves the user's avatar from Gravatar by using an image URL based on a hash of the email address. Websites, including Bullhorn, may freely use Gravatar to display the user's image. Bullhorn displays the image next to posts and on the profile page.

```
<img src="https://www.gravatar.com/avatar/205e460b479e2e5b48aec
07710c08d50?s=150"/>
```

To control the size of the image, append the URL with `?s=150` where 150 is the height or width in pixels of the square image to be returned by the URL. The value of 's' can range from 1 to 2048. Lower values will look better.

D. Wolf and A.J. Henley, *Java EE Web Application Primer*,
https://doi.org/10.1007/978-1-4842-3195-1_19

If a user does not have a Gravatar set up then a default image will be displayed:

`https://www.gravatar.com/avatar/unknownhash`

Calculating an MD5 Hash with Java

An MD5 hash is a way of encrypting text such that it is not identifiable by looking at it. The value of MD5 is that the same email address will always generate the same MD5 hash.

The Gravatar URL is made from an MD5 hash of the user's email address. You can create an MD5 hash of an email address using code provided at the Gravatar website. This code is implemented in Bullhorn in the `MD5Util.java` class. The code will return a string containing the MD5 hash given the user's email address.[1]

The `DbUser` class in Bullhorn contains a method that generates the Gravatar URL. The method takes two parameters, email and image size. The method then returns the correct URL, which can be used in an image tag throughout the Bullhorn site. See Listing 19-1.

[1]The source code for the MD5 class in Bullhorn is derived from that found at `http://en.gravatar.com/site/implement/images/java`.

Listing 19-1. The Method to Generate a Gravatar URL Based on the User's Email Address

```
public static String getGravatarURL(String email, Integer size)
{
                StringBuilder url = new StringBuilder();
                url.append("http://www.gravatar.com/avatar/");
                url.append(MD5Util.md5Hex(email));
                url.append("?s=" + size.toString());
                return url.toString();
        }
```

CHAPTER 20

The Presentation/View

The presentation layer, also known as the view, is the perspective your end user has of your application. They don't see all the Java code. They only see what the browser displays. The view consists mostly of HTML, JavaScript, and images. In this section, we'll look at the different JSP files that make up the view. The JSP files contain other code such as JSTL, but the end result is that they become HTML files sent to the user's browser.

To start, the user browses to the site's URL for the `login.jsp` page. The URL for your development environment will be `http://localhost:8080/Bullhorn/login.jsp`.

Note To start your application in Eclipse, at the login page simply right-click on the login page and select the option to Run on Server. Your site will open in a browser inside the Eclipse environment.

The Code for the Login Page

```
<!-- login.jsp -->
<%@ page language="java" contentType="text/html;
    charset=UTF-8" pageEncoding="UTF-8"%>
<!DOCTYPE html PUBLIC "-//W3C//DTD HTML 4.01 Transitional//EN"
"http://www.w3.org/TR/html4/loose.dtd">
<html>
<head>
```


D. Wolf and A.J. Henley, *Java EE Web Application Primer*,
https://doi.org/10.1007/978-1-4842-3195-1_20

```
<meta http-equiv="Content-Type" content="text/html;
charset=UTF-8"/>
<jsp:include page="bootstrap.jsp"></jsp:include>
  </head>
  <body>
    <h1>Login</h1>

    <div class="container">
      <form class="form-signin" method="post"
      action="LoginServlet">
        <h2 class="form-signin-heading">${message}Please sign
        in</h2>
        <label for="inputEmail" class="sr-only">Email address
        </label>
        <input name="email" type="email" id="inputEmail"
        class="form-control"
        placeholder="Email address" required autofocus>
        <input type="hidden" name="action" id="action"
        value="login"/>
        <label for="inputPassword" class="sr-only">Password
        </label>
        <input name="password"  type="password"
        id="inputPassword"
        class="form-control" placeholder="Password" required>

        <button class="btn btn-lg btn-primary btn-block"
        type="submit">Sign in</button>
      </form>
    <a href="adduser.jsp">Join</a>
    </div> <!-- /container -->

<jsp:include page="footer.jsp"></jsp:include>
</body>
</html>
```

The Code for the Home Page

```
<!-- home.jsp -->
<%@ page language="java" contentType="text/html;
    charset=UTF-8" pageEncoding="UTF-8"%>
<!DOCTYPE html PUBLIC "-//W3C//DTD HTML 4.01 Transitional//EN"
"http://www.w3.org/TR/html4/loose.dtd">
<html>
<head>
<meta http-equiv="Content-Type" content="text/html;
charset=UTF-8"/>
<title>Bullhorn</title>
<jsp:include page="bootstrap.jsp"></jsp:include>
</head>
<body>
<jsp:include page="navbar.jsp"></jsp:include>
<h1>This is the home page</h1>
<form role="form" action="PostServ" method="post"
onsubmit="return validate(this);">
                <div class="form-group">
                    <label for="post">Create New Post (141
                    char):</label>
                    <textarea name= "posttext" id="posttext"
                    class="form-control" rows="2" placeholder=
                    "Express yourself!" maxlength="141"></textarea>
                    <div id="textarea_feedback"></div>
                    </div>
                    <div class = "form-group">
                    <input type="submit" value="Submit"
                    id="submit"/>
                    <input type="reset" value="Clear"/>
                </div>
            </form>
```

```
<jsp:include page="footer.jsp"></jsp:include>
<script>
$(document).ready(function() {
    var text_max = 141;
    $('#textarea_feedback').html(text_max + ' characters
    remaining');

    $('#posttext').keyup(function() {
        var text_length = $('#posttext').val().length;
        var text_remaining = text_max - text_length;

        $('#textarea_feedback').html(text_remaining + '
        characters remaining');
    });
});

function validate(form) {
        valid = true;
        if ($('#posttext').val().length==0){
                alert("You may not submit an empty post.");
                valid = false;
        }
        return valid;
}
</script>
</body>
</html>
```

The Code for the News Feed Page

```
<!-- newsfeed.jsp -->
<%@ page language="java" contentType="text/html;
    charset=UTF-8" pageEncoding="UTF-8"%>
```

```
<%@ taglib prefix="c" uri="http://java.sun.com/jsp/jstl/core" %>
<%@ taglib prefix="fmt" uri="http://java.sun.com/jsp/jstl/fmt" %>
<fmt:setLocale value="en_US" /><!-- fixes date not displaying
correctly in Eclipse browser -->
<!DOCTYPE html PUBLIC "-//W3C//DTD HTML 4.01 Transitional//EN"
"http://www.w3.org/TR/html4/loose.dtd">
<html>
<head>
<meta http-equiv="Content-Type" content="text/html;
charset=UTF-8"/>
<title>BullHorn</title>
<jsp:include page="bootstrap.jsp"></jsp:include>
</head>
<body>
<jsp:include page="navbar.jsp"></jsp:include>
<h1>This is the news feed page</h1>
<div class="container">
<table class="table table-bordered">
    <thead>
        <tr><th>User</th><th>Post</th><th>Date</th></tr>
    </thead>
    <tbody>
    <c:forEach var="post" items="${posts}">
        <tr><td><a href="ProfileServlet?action=viewprofile&user
        id=<c:out value="${post.bhuser.bhuserid}"/>">
        <c:out value="${post.bhuser.useremail}"/></a></td>
        <td><c:out value="${post.posttext}"/></td>
        <td><fmt:formatDate value="${post.postdate}"
        pattern="yy-MMM-dd"/></td>
        </tr>
```

```
    </c:forEach>
    </tbody>
    </table>

</div>

<jsp:include page="footer.jsp"></jsp:include>
</body>
```

The Code for the Profile Page

```
</html>
<!-- profile.jsp -->
<%@ page language="java" contentType="text/html;
    charset=UTF-8" pageEncoding="UTF-8"%>
<%@ taglib prefix="c" uri="http://java.sun.com/jsp/jstl/core" %>
<%@ taglib prefix="fmt" uri="http://java.sun.com/jsp/jstl/fmt" %>
<!DOCTYPE html PUBLIC "-//W3C//DTD HTML 4.01 Transitional//EN"
"http://www.w3.org/TR/html4/loose.dtd">
<html>
<head>
<meta http-equiv="Content-Type" content="text/html;
charset=UTF-8"/>
<title>BullHorn</title>
<jsp:include page="bootstrap.jsp"></jsp:include>
</head>
<body>
<jsp:include page="navbar.jsp"></jsp:include>
```

```
<c:choose>
        <c:when test="${editProfile==false}">
                <h1><img src="${userimage}" alt=<c:out value="
                ${username}"/>/>  Profile for <c:out
                value="${username}"/></h1>
                <h2>Email: <c:out value="${useremail}"/></h2>
                <h2>Motto: <c:out value="${usermotto}"/></h2>
                <h2>Join Date: <c:out
                value="${userjoindate}"/></h2>
        </c:when>
        <c:when test="${editProfile==true}">
        <h1><img src="${userimage}" alt="${username}"/> &n
        bsp;Edit Profile for ${username}</h1>
                <form action="ProfileServlet" method="post">
                        <input type="hidden" name="action"
                        value="updateprofile">
                        <input type="hidden" name="userid"
                        value="${userid}">
                        <h2>Email: <input
                        type="text" name="useremail"
                        value="${useremail}"/></h2>
                        <h2>Motto: <input
                        type="text" name="usermotto"
                        value="${usermotto}"/></h2>
                        <h2>Join Date: <c:out
                        value="${userjoindate}"/></h2>
                        <input type="submit" value="Save
                        Changes"/>
                </form>
        </c:when>
</c:choose>
```

```
<jsp:include page="footer.jsp"></jsp:include>
</body>
</html>
```

The Code for the Add User Page

```
<!-- adduser.jsp -->
<%@ page language="java" contentType="text/html;
    charset=UTF-8" pageEncoding="UTF-8"%>
<%@ taglib prefix="c" uri="http://java.sun.com/jsp/jstl/core" %>
<%@ taglib prefix="fmt" uri="http://java.sun.com/jsp/jstl/fmt" %>
<fmt:setLocale value="en_US" /><!-- fixes date not displaying
correctly in Eclipse browser -->
<!DOCTYPE html PUBLIC "-//W3C//DTD HTML 4.01 Transitional//EN"
"http://www.w3.org/TR/html4/loose.dtd">
<html>
<head>
<meta http-equiv="Content-Type" content="text/html;
charset=UTF-8"/>
<title>BullHorn</title>
<jsp:include page="bootstrap.jsp"></jsp:include>
</head>
<body>

<form action="AddUser" method="post">
    <input type="hidden" name="action" value="addUser">
        <h1>Add New User</h1>
        <h2>Name: <input type="text" name="userName"
        value=""/></h2>
        <h2>Email: <input type="text" name="userEmail"
        value=""/></h2>
```

```
        <h2>Password: <input type="password"
        name="userPassword" value=""/></h2>
        <h2>Motto: <input type="text" name="userMotto"
        value=""/></h2>
        <!-- <h2>Join Date: <input type="text" value=""/></h2>-->
        <input type="submit" value="Join Us"/>
</form>

<jsp:include page="footer.jsp"></jsp:include>
</body>
</html>
```

The Code for the Support Page

```
<!-- support.jsp -->
<%@ page language="java" contentType="text/html;
    charset=UTF-8" pageEncoding="UTF-8"%>
<!DOCTYPE html PUBLIC "-//W3C//DTD HTML 4.01 Transitional//EN"
"http://www.w3.org/TR/html4/loose.dtd">
<html>
<head>
<meta http-equiv="Content-Type" content="text/html;
charset=UTF-8"/>
<title>BullHorn</title>
<jsp:include page="bootstrap.jsp"></jsp:include>
</head>
<body>
<jsp:include page="navbar.jsp"></jsp:include>

<h1>This is the support page</h1>
<jsp:include page="footer.jsp"></jsp:include>
</body>
</html>
```

The Code for the Error Page

```
<!-- error.jsp -->
<%@ page language="java" contentType="text/html;
   charset=UTF-8" pageEncoding="UTF-8"%>
<!DOCTYPE html PUBLIC "-//W3C//DTD HTML 4.01 Transitional//EN"
"http://www.w3.org/TR/html4/loose.dtd">
<html>
<head>
<meta http-equiv="Content-Type" content="text/html;
charset=UTF-8"/>
<title>BullHorn</title>
<jsp:include page="bootstrap.jsp"></jsp:include>
</head>
<body>
<jsp:include page="navbar.jsp"></jsp:include>

        <div style="text-align:center">
                <h1>Something's Wrong...</h1>
        </div>

<jsp:include page="footer.jsp"></jsp:include>
</body>
</html>
```

The Navbar Include File

```
<!-- begin navbar -->
<nav class="navbar navbar-default">
  <div class="container-fluid">
    <!-- Brand and toggle get grouped for better mobile
    display -->
```

```
<div class="navbar-header">
  <button type="button" class="navbar-toggle collapsed"
  data-toggle="collapse" data-target="#bs-example-navbar-
  collapse-1" aria-expanded="false">
    <span class="sr-only">Toggle navigation</span>
  </button>
  <img src="images/bullhornlogo50x50.png" alt="Bullhorn
  Logo"/> <h2>Bullhorn</h2>
</div>

<!-- Collect the nav links, forms, and other content for
toggling -->
<div class="collapse navbar-collapse" id="bs-example-
navbar-collapse-1">

  <ul class="nav navbar-nav">
    <li class="active"><a href="home.jsp">Home<span
    class="sr-only">(current)</span></a></li>
    <li><a href="Newsfeed">News Feed</a></li>
  </ul>

  <form class="navbar-form navbar-right" role="search"
  action="Newsfeed" method="get">
    <div class="form-group">
      <input type="text" class="form-control"
      placeholder="Search" name="searchtext">
    </div>
    <button type="submit" class="btn btn-default">Submit
    </button>
  </form>

  <ul class="nav navbar-nav navbar-right">
  <% if (session.getAttribute("user") != null) { %>
```

```
        <li><a href="ProfileServlet?userid=${user.bhuserid}&act
        ion=viewprofile"><img alt="${user.username}" src="${gra
        vatarURL}"/> ${user.username}</a></li>
      <% } %>
        <li class="dropdown">
          <a href="#" class="dropdown-toggle"
          data-toggle="dropdown" role="button"
          aria-haspopup="true" aria-expanded="false">User
          Options <span class="caret"></span></a>
          <ul class="dropdown-menu">
            <li>
              <!-- <li><a href="LoginServlet?action=logout">Log
              out</a></li>-->
              <!-- Bootstrap allows me to put a form here and
              it will show in the navbar.
                   I want to use a form so it can call the
                   servlet with the Post method.
               -->
               <form class="navbar-form navbar-left"
               role="form" action="LoginServlet" method="post">
                  <input type="hidden" name="action"
                  id="action" value="logout"/>
                  <button class="btn btn-default"
                  id="addBookButton">Logout</button>
               </form>
            </li>
            <li><a href="Newsfeed?userid=${user.bhuserid }">
            Show my Posts</a></li>
            <li><a href="ProfileServlet?userid=${user.bhuserid }
            &action=editprofile">Edit Profile</a></li>
            <li role="separator" class="divider"></li>
            <li><a href="support.jsp">Feedback</a></li>
```

```
          </ul>
        </li>
      </ul>
    </div><!-- /.navbar-collapse -->
  </div><!-- /.container-fluid -->
</nav>
<!--  end navbar -->
```

The BootStrap Include File

The BootStrap include file contains links for the BootStrap files. These links come from the BootStrap website. They use a content delivery service called MaxCDN to host their files. You don't have to download anything. Simply include the links from the BootStrap site, and your application will retrieve the file over the internet.

The BootStrap include file also contains links to some style sheets, which can be found in the styles folder of your Bullhorn application. The styles folder lies below the WebContent folder.

```
<!-- BEGIN Bootstrap -->
<link href="//maxcdn.bootstrapcdn.com/bootstrap/3.3.1/css/
bootstrap.min.css" rel="stylesheet">
<!-- jQuery (necessary for BootStrap's JavaScript plugins) -->
<script src="https://ajax.googleapis.com/ajax/libs/
jquery/1.11.1/jquery.min.js"></script>
<!-- Include all compiled plugins (below), or include
individual files as needed -->
<script src="//maxcdn.bootstrapcdn.com/bootstrap/3.3.1/js/
bootstrap.min.js"></script>
<link href="styles/cerulean.bootstrap.min.css" rel="stylesheet">
<link href="styles/bullhorn.css" rel="stylesheet">
<!-- END Bootstrap -->
```

The Bootstrap Style Pages

The Bullhorn site contains some style sheets that have been downloaded from `https://bootswatch.com/`. This site contains free downloadable BootStrap themes that you can include in your projects. Simply browse their collection and include them in your site. Then, from each web page, you need to include a link to the theme you want to use. This is done in the BootStrap include file.

The Footer Include File

```
<!--footer.jsp-->
  <div id="push"></div>
  <div id="footer">
      <div class="container">
        <p class="text-muted"><span class="glyphicon
        glyphicon-volume-up" aria-hidden="true"> 
        Bullhorn  &copy; 2016</span></p>
       </div>
   </div>
<!-- end footer.jsp -->
```

Index

D. Wolf and A.J. Henley, *Java EE Web Application Primer*,
https://doi.org/10.1007/978-1-4842-3195-1

D

E

F

G

H

I

J, K

R

S

T

U

V

W, X, Y, Z

Printed in the United States
By Bookmasters